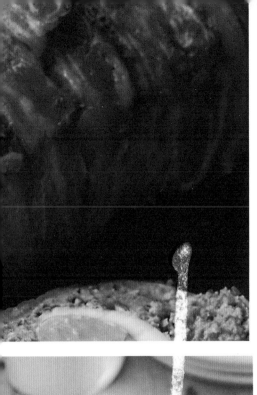

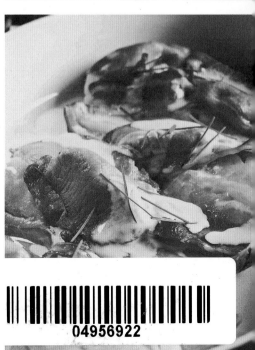

THE BACON
COOKBOOK

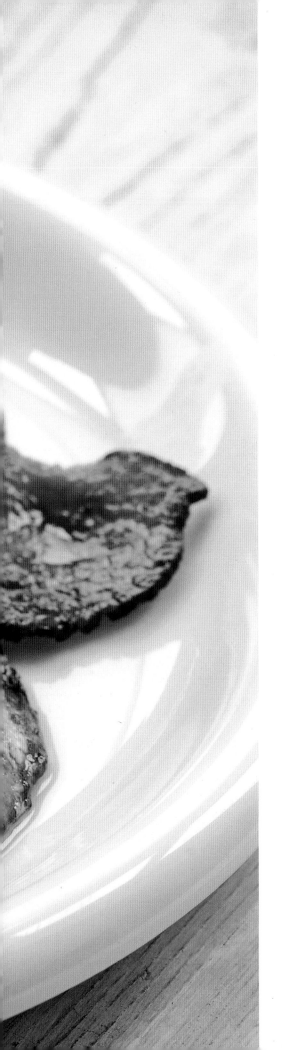

THE BACON COOKBOOK

More than just breakfast – 50 irresistible
recipes for all-day eating

CAROL WILSON

LORENZ BOOKS

CONTENTS

INTRODUCTION

Whether you prefer it smoked or unsmoked, fatty, lean, salty, mild, crisp or chewy, bacon is quick and easy to cook and wonderfully versatile. Its rich, savoury flavour is delicious just on its own, although the addition of bacon to stews, soups, salads, vegetables, pasta, rice, fish and meat dishes perks up them up and elevates them from the ordinary into something special.

The enticing aroma of sizzling bacon is simply irresistible, making it one of the world's most popular foods. In fact, apart from its enduring appeal in the traditional kitchen, everyone has recently gone mad for bacon, with a variety of bacon-flavoured products that include beer, vodka, brownies, jam, fudge, ice cream, cupcakes, chocolate and even bacon-flavoured toothpaste!

Bacon is indisputably one of the finest and most versatile cuts of pork, which has had a devoted following of epicurean meat-lovers for hundreds of years.

Above *Pork loin is by far the most popular cut of meat for curing to make bacon.*

Below *Tamworth pigs have been reared for bacon production for many centuries.*

A HISTORY OF BACON

Pigs have been reared domestically for their mouthwatering meat for many hundreds of years. The word 'bacon' means 'meat from the back of an animal' and is thought to come from the prehistoric German word '*bak*' and the French word '*bako*'. The Chinese were preserving pork bellies in salt as far back as 1500BC, and in Roman Britain, the Romans recognized bacon as *petaso*, which they boiled with dried figs, browned over the fire and served with sauce. Bacon as we know it today has been available since the early 17th century.

Bacon comes from the side, belly, back and loin of the pig and is made by curing (preserving) and sometimes smoking the meat. There's a variety of cuts: streaky (fatty), from the belly, which is quite fatty with layers of fat running parallel to the rind; middle, which is cut from the side of the pig and streaked with fat but leaner than streaky; and back, which has less fat than either.

Slab bacon comes from the belly and side cuts of the pig, and is typically very high in fat. Collar (neck) is more ususally cooked as a joint for boiling or braising (for which it is excellent, although it must be well soaked before cooking), can also be sliced into strips. Bacon chops are cut from the collar, shoulder or back.

Bacon may be smoked or unsmoked – the latter is termed 'green' and is paler and milder than smoked. In England a side of unsliced bacon is traditionally termed a flitch, and an individual slice of bacon was once known as a collop but is now called a rasher. In North America a side of bacon is a slab and a piece of bacon is called a slice.

Breeding Pigs for Bacon

Originally, pigs for bacon were heavier than pigs for fresh pork, and were chosen for their ability to produce enormous sides of bacon. Some breeds such as the Yorkshire and the Tamworth were specially bred purely for bacon. Pigs intended for bacon are still killed today at a heavier weight than those for fresh pork, usually at around 100 kilos/220 lbs.

Pigs were born in the spring and either fattened on acorns from oak forests or allowed into the orchard to graze on fallen apples. After slaughtering, the pig would be hung for a day and then cured with salt. The cure might be dry (salt) or wet (brine) and could be sweet (with honey), spiced or plain. Each family would have their own recipe, handed down from generation to generation. Sides of bacon, glistening with salt were hung from the rafters to mature and later could be hung in the chimney and smoked, which preserved the meat.

Historically, a pig was the most sought-after prize at summer fairs in England where competitors were invited to chase a greased pig. The winner was given the pig to take home – one of the possible roots of the saying 'to bring home the bacon'.

The Dunmow Flitch Trials

Bacon features prominently in an ancient English custom that still takes place every four years in Great Dunmow in Essex. A flitch of bacon is awarded to married couples from anywhere in the world if they can satisfy the Judge and Jury of 'six maidens and six bachelors' that in 'twelvemonth and a day' they have 'not wisht themselves unmarried again'.

It is believed to have originated in 1104 at the Augustinian Priory of Little Dunmow when the Lord of the Manor, Reginald Fitzwalter and his wife, dressed as poor people, asked the blessing of the Prior a year and a day after their marriage. The Prior was so delighted by their devotion that he presented them with a flitch of bacon. After the Reformation the custom lapsed, but was revived in 1855 and the Trials were again staged in Great Dunmow and have been held regularly ever since. A flitch of bacon is ceremoniously carried through the streets, held high by the flitch bearers. Then, consenting couples are carried shoulder-high by the bearers in the ancient Flitch Chair to the Market Place to take their oath.

An American Way of Life

The first pigs were brought to America by Hernando de Soto in 1539. Just three years later his original herd of 13 pigs had grown to many hundreds. The pork revolution had started in earnest, with pig production spreading rapidly through the new colonies. In the great Western expansion at the end of the nineteenth century cured bacon was essential to the many thousands of prospectors, settlers and explorers who relied on its sustenance, with the bacon fat being used to fry up root vegetables over the camp fire. As herds increased, meat processing centres set up in major towns across the country, although getting your pigs to market was no mean feat, with drovers driving their herds hundreds of miles to be sold. However, in 1887 Swift & Co introduced the refrigerated railroad car which meant that processed pork could be shipped instead of live pigs.

The commercial success of bacon, however, was sealed by the invention of Oscar F Mayer, a German immigrant, who perfected a method of slicing and packaging bacon in the 1920s. This revolutionized the way that bacon could be sold and transported around the country, making sure that every American could look forward to their sliced and packed bacon at breakfast. It became a staple food during the Great Depression and bacon fat was the main cooking oil used throughout the second world war.

Bacon has continued to grow in popularity on both sides of the Atlantic with a recent trend away from mass-produced bacon towards small farms selling their own cured and smoked bacon. Some of the older, fattier heritage breeds such as the Tamworth, the Large Black and the Old Spot are now being bred for their more rewarding bacon meat.

Above *Every four years the flitch bearers of Great Dunmow parade a flitch of bacon through the streets. It is then presented to the couple who swear their continuing allegiance to each other.*

Below *Traditionally, hanging bacon up in smoke-filled kitchen rafters would cure the meat, preserving it for the long winter months ahead.*

Bacon is popular across the globe, although which part of the pig it comes from and how it is cured and smoked varies from country to country.

Above Pancetta stesa *is similar in appearance to streaky (fatty) bacon (known throughout the UK and America), but the curing process produces a different flavour with the emphasis on herbs and spices.*

Below left Ventrèche *is dry-cured with herbs and spices.*

Below right Speck *is used throughout Northern Europe to enhance the flavour of soups and stews.*

INTERNATIONAL TYPES OF BACON

Italy
Italian pancetta comes from the belly of the pig (*pancia*) and is similar to streaky bacon, but has a completely different flavour as it is cured in a different way. Pancetta is salt-cured, salted and spiced, often with fennel, pepper and nutmeg, and is an important ingredient of many Italian dishes. *Pancetta curata* is air-dried or salt-cured; *pancetta arrotolata* (rolled pancetta) is lean and spiced with peppercorns and cloves; *pancetta stesa* is the belly left flat, like bacon, and *pancetta affumicata* is smoked.

France
The French word for bacon is *lard* or *lardons* if diced (derived from the Latin word for bacon fat *lardum*). A rasher of bacon is called a *tranche de lard*; streaky bacon is known as *lard de poitrine* or if smoked, as *poitrine fumée*; very lean bacon is called bacon.

Ventrèche (which means belly) from southwest France is similar to Italian pancetta and comes from the part of the pig's belly where the muscles are separated by strips of fat. Like pancetta, it is cured rather than smoked and is meatier than bacon.

Germany
Bacon in Germany is similar to streaky bacon and is known generally as *speck*. Speck is popular in all German-speaking countries and in Slovak cuisine. *Bauchspeck* comes from the belly and is marbled with muscle and fat. After curing it is smoked over beech wood and used for cooking. Bauchspeck is usually sold in pieces with the '*schwarte*' (rind) removed. In southwest Austria bauchspeck is air-cured and smoked over birch wood. *Schinkenspeck* is a cured and smoked cut of pork from the back hip which is sliced thinly and usually served cold. It has larger muscles and less marbling than the less expensive speck used for cooking. Black Forest (*Schwarzwald*) bacon is a speciality that is cured in spiced brine, then smoked over pine wood, until black on the outside.

Spain

The Spanish term for bacon is *tocino*, which is mostly unsmoked; if smoked it is usually called bacon. *Tocino Iberico* is a gourmet bacon, made from pigs fed on acorns. Another type of Spanish bacon is *tocino de pancetta*, pork belly that has been salt-cured, salted and spiced, then dried for about three months. It is very fatty with very little meat.

Great Britain

Back bacon is the most widely used bacon cut in the UK and is primarily served for breakfast. Streaky bacon is used either chopped up as a garnish or to wrap around meat to help retain moisture.

Netherlands

In the Netherlands *Zeeuws spek* is cut from the belly, seasoned with salt, pepper and bay leaf, then marinated in spicy oil and mustard. It is generally sold lightly grilled rather than as raw meat.

Eastern Europe

In Hungary, *szalona*, a substantial slab bacon, is more fat than meat and is smoked. Originally it was a peasant's meal, when pieces of szalona were placed on sticks and held over an open fire, until the fat melted and the hot fat was spread onto salted rye bread. Gypsy bacon (*ciganyszalonna*), a reddish-coloured paprika-coated spicy bacon, has more meat and is served thinly sliced with rye bread and raw onion or raw garlic, or sliced and fried, and added to stews and soups for added flavour. The Polish version is *boczek*, which is brined and then smoked.

USA and Canada

American bacon is cut from the belly into very thin strips, is reasonably fatty and is usually smoked after curing. It varies in flavour according to the cure; red pepper, sugar, maple sugar or syrup, honey and molasses are popularly used in American cures. It is usually cooked in a pan in its own fat until golden and crisp.

Canadian bacon (or Canadian-style bacon) comes from the loin from the back of the pig. It is less fatty than American-style bacon and is usually smoked. Peameal or cornmeal bacon is another type of Canadian bacon which is different from standard bacon as it is brined rather than smoked. Traditionally, the cured piece of bacon was rolled in ground dried yellow peas to keep it dry and preserve it, although today yellow cornmeal is used instead. It was developed in Toronto around 1875 by English immigrant William Davies.

Australia and New Zealand

Middle bacon is the most common variety sold in strips in Australia and New Zealand, although leaner cuts from the loin section are also sold in supermarkets. This is sold as 'short cut bacon'.

Above *In Spanish homes, the fat from* tocino de pancetta *is used traditionally used to cook onions and garlic, and is extremely flavoursome.*

Above *Canadian peameal bacon is wet-cured and then coated in the distinctive yellow cornmeal .*

Below *Most American bacon is sold in thin strips to fry, grill (broil), or bake before serving.*

Curing ensures that the bacon will keep without refrigeration. The practice dates back to the ancient world when salting was the only way to keep the flesh of animals for any length of time without spoiling. Salt draws out moisture, preserves the meat and also adds flavour.

Above *Bacon that has been cured in brine generally has a darker appearance than a simple dry cure.*

Below *Traditionally, Wiltshire-cured bacon would be hung and left to mature for two weeks in a cool cellar.*

CURING AND SMOKING

Bacon may be wet- or dry-cured. Wet-cured bacon is cured in a brine tub with salt, sodium nitrate, spices, sugar and seasonings. Other liquids may also be added, e.g. apple juice, cider or ale. Some manufacturers also inject the brine into the meat to increase the weight and volume; however, bacon that's been cured in this way will shrink and release a milky liquid when it's cooked, and won't be as crisp as dry-cured.

Dry-cured bacon is classically rubbed with a mixture of dry salt, sodium nitrate, spices and sometimes herbs and then hung to dry and mature. This removes water so that the bacon shrinks less during cooking and prevents 'white bits' in the pan.

The type of salt used for curing is important. Coarse salt is best as it dissolves more slowly and permeates the meat. Fine salt would seal the meat too quickly before it could penetrate the flesh. Saltpetre (potassium nitrate) is used to kill bacteria and also gives bacon its pink colour.

For hundreds of years, country dwellers and farmers had their own secret recipes for curing and smoking bacon. Before sugar became affordable, honey was a popular ingredient as it had the ability to seep into the meat quickly. Other ingredients might include beer, cider, mustard, treacle, vinegar, aromatic spices and herbs.

The Wiltshire Cure

Whether it is dry or wet, the cure is of singular importance to the flavour of the finished product. Indeed many commercial producers still have their own secret curing recipes today. Earlier cures from 100 years ago would be too salty for modern tastes, so contemporary cures are milder than those of the past. In England, the types of cure would vary according to region and were distinctively different in flavour and texture. Some English cures such as the Wiltshire Cure have become world famous.

The Wiltshire Cure was developed by the Harris family of Calne in the 1840s and was revolutionary at the time, as the meat was cured in rooms chilled by ice. As meat keeps fresh for longer at lower temperatures, the Harris family discovered that much less salt was needed to cure their bacon and so a milder cure was possible. The meat is immersed in brine for three to four days, then put into a cool cellar for two weeks to mature, before smoking over oak, pine or beech wood for two to three days.

Suffolk Sweet-Cured Bacon is dry-cured with salt and molasses sugar for six weeks, then smoked over oak; the deep pink salty bacon has a rich treacly flavour.

Ayrshire bacon from southwest Scotland is a very lightly salted mild cure that originated in 1857 and is still very popular throughout Scotland. After curing, the rind is removed and the meat is tightly rolled and tied with string, which ensures that the fat and lean meat are evenly distributed, before it is cut into rashers. It may be smoked or unsmoked.

American bacon is often dry-cured using maple syrup and molasses for a heightened sweet flavour, then smoked over hickory or cherry wood chips. There are now numerous local bacon producers all over the United States producing their own signature bacon ranges with a highly inventive list of curing ingredients.

Mass-produced bacon comes from intensively reared pigs which have almost no exercise, and are fed on a low fat diet. Consequently, bacon from these pigs has far less flavour than that from free-range outdoor pigs. Their meat is usually 'cured' by being injected with brine and phosphates to plump it up and increase its weight, but as a consequence, during cooking it exudes white liquid and shrinks a great deal in the pan. It is worth paying more for traditionally cured bacon, smoked in the age-old way to guarantee the best flavour and texture.

Smoked bacon

After curing, bacon can be smoked to further enhance the flavour. Wood chippings are usually used; oak, beech, apple and hickory wood are the most popular. The choice of wood is an important factor in the taste of the bacon. The tarry substances in wood smoke also kill bacteria and form an airtight seal on the surface, while the smoke penetrates the meat to impart a distinctive smoky flavour. Some North American bacon makers also smoke bacon over burning corncobs. Nowadays, cold smoking in a kiln or smokehouse is done at a temperature below 30°C (86°F) to avoid cooking the meat, but which allows the bacon to change in colour, flavour and texture. Smoking gives a dark golden hue to the bacon rind too.

These days some large-scale commercially smoked bacon is produced in smoking factories, with less smoking time than the traditional product (to reduce weight loss) and the use of dyes to replicate the appearance of bacon smoked for a longer period. Bacon described as 'smoke flavour' has a chemical added to give a smoky flavour, instead of being smoked in the traditional way.

Above Smoking bacon slowly over apple, hickory or cherry wood chips enhances the flavour of the meat.

Below An old-fashioned smokehouse at Quiet Valley Historical Farm, Pennsylvania, USA.

It's not difficult to make bacon at home. A piece of belly, loin or shoulder pork weighing from 1-5 kg/2¼-3 pounds is ideal. Make sure all utensils are scrupulously clean and sterilized and that the room is as cool as possible.

MAKING YOUR OWN BACON

OTHER DRY-CURE MIXES
It is worth experimenting with different herbs and spices to really get the perfect mix for your own taste.

Spicy dry-cure mixture:
1 kg/2¼lb pork belly or loin
50g/2 oz coarse salt
50g/2 oz granulated (white) sugar
½g saltpetre
5ml/1 tsp light brown sugar
5ml/1 tsp crushed juniper berries
5ml/1tsp mustard powder

Herbal dry-cure mixture:
50g/2 oz coarse salt
50g/2 oz granulated (white) sugar
½g saltpetre
5ml/1 tsp muscovado sugar
5ml/1 tsp cracked peppercorns
5ml/1 tsp ground coriander
5ml/1 tsp freshly grated nutmeg
5ml/1 tsp finely chopped
   bay leaf
5ml/1 tsp chopped rosemary
5ml/1 tsp chopped thyme

It's important to use the correct type of salt – coarse rock or sea salt. Special curing salt is also available and is a combination of salt and sodium nitrite or sodium nitrate. It's sometimes coloured pink to differentiate it from ordinary salt.

For dry curing you'll need about 30g/2 tbsp of salt for every kilo/2¼lb of meat (the salt can draw up to 26% of moisture from the meat), half a gram of saltpetre (a preservative which gives bacon its pink colour and flavour) and 15-30g/1-2 tbsp of sugar if you prefer a sweeter bacon. A higher amount of sugar gives a sweetcure. You can also add dried herbs (10g/2 tsp per kilo/2¼lb of meat), spices, honey and molasses.

Dry Curing Bacon
This simple recipe is a good one to try at first and will produce a wonderful flavour.

1 kg/2¼lb pork belly or loin
40g/1½ oz coarse salt
40g/1½ oz curing salt
½g saltpetre
20g/¾ oz light muscovado sugar
20g/¾ oz thyme, chopped

1 You can either remove the rind or leave it on (it will take a little longer to cure with the rind). Pierce the thicker part of the meat on both sides, including the rind, with a skewer to help the cure to penetrate. Mix together the salts, saltpetre, sugar and thyme.

2 Rub the mixture well into the pork belly. Use your fingers to really rub the mixture into all the crevices in the meat.

3 Put the meat flesh side down into a large plastic food bag. You could also use a non-metallic container, such as a plastic coolbox. Cover and put into the refrigerator or cold room and turn the meat every day, rubbing in the cure mixture, for 2-6 days – a liquid will form in the base of the bag or container. Pour off the liquid as it forms.

4 Rinse the meat well and pat dry. Wrap the meat in muslin (cheese-cloth) and refrigerate for 1-2 days to dry. A pellicle (shiny thin skin) will form on the surface. The pellicle prevents the fat in the meat from rising to the surface and spoiling; it also seals in moisture, preventing the bacon from drying out entirely and providing a surface to which smoke molecules will cling better.

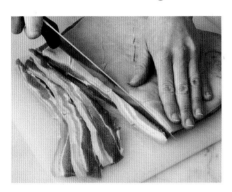

5 If you are not going to smoke the bacon, it is now ready to slice and cook. Don't worry if a powdery white mould has appeared – this is harmless, but can be removed by wiping it off with a cloth soaked in vinegar.

Wet Curing Bacon

This method is quicker than dry curing. The meat is soaked in salted water with or without spices. Use spring water, as tap water is treated with chemicals which can interfere with the curing process.

1 kg/2¼lb pork belly or loin
375g/12 oz coarse salt
6 peppercorns
6 bay leaves
1 onion, quartered
1 sprig rosemary
450 ml/16 fl oz/scant 2 cups maple syrup or honey
600 ml/20 fl oz/2½ cups water

SMOKING BACON

If you want to smoke your bacon, it is important that the cured meat is completely dry, otherwise the smoke won't penetrate.

Home smokers are widely available. Bacon should be cold-smoked at a temperature of around 30°C/86°F. Higher temperatures will cook the meat,

while lower temperatures might promote bacterial growth. You can buy packs of different wood sawdusts to vary the taste of the smoked bacon.

Smoke for at least 5 hours (or much longer if you prefer a pronounced smoky flavour) or until the internal temperature of the meat reaches 65°C/150°F. It can then be sliced as required.

1 Put all the ingredients into a pan and bring to a boil, stirring. Remove from the heat and leave to cool for 1 hour.

2 Strain the liquid. Place the meat in a non-metallic container with enough room to cover by at least 3cm/1½ in of the strained liquid.

3 Pour the liquid over the meat and weigh the meat down with a plate or non-metallic weight so that it is submerged under the liquid. Cover and refrigerate for 4 days. Remove the meat from the liquid and pat dry.

4 The bacon is now ready to slice. Cook immediately or divide into sections, wrap in cling film (plastic wrap) and freeze.

Fresh bacon should not smell of anything and should feel slightly damp, not dry, wet or slimy. The meat should be firm with a deep pink colour and there should be no green shimmering parts on the flesh. The fat should be firm and white, although the fat of smoked bacon may be slightly yellow.

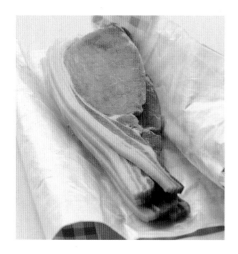

Above *Keep raw bacon wrapped up in the refrigerator and out of contact with any other food items.*

Below left *Frying bacon is quick and easy, and smells irresistible.*

Below right *Grilling bacon allows the excess fat to drop through to the grill tray below.*

COOKING WITH BACON

Freshly sliced bacon should be used within 2 days. Pre-packed unsmoked bacon should be used within 7 days of opening (smoked bacon will keep for 10 days), but may be kept for up to 1 month unopened (check the use-by date). Bacon joints will keep for 3 days. Ready packaged bacon should be stored in the refrigerator. Once opened, rewrap in cling film (plastic wrap) or greaseproof paper and eat by the use-by date.

You can also store cooked bacon. Cook the bacon slightly below its normal cooking level. Drain on absorbent kitchen paper and leave to cool. Wrap tightly in foil or cling film and refrigerate for up to 5 days.

Bacon freezes well and should be defrosted overnight in the refrigerator. Rashers should be divided into portions, and placed in freezer bags with as much air as possible expelled and tightly wrapped. To freeze packs of unopened bacon, overwrap the pack tightly with heavy duty foil and use within 2 months. Joints can also be frozen. Wrap in cling film then heavy-duty foil, ensuring it is airtight, and freeze.

Cooked bacon can also be frozen. Wrap individual portions in cling film or foil and place in a freezer bag.

Cooking Methods

Starting in a cold pan reduces shrinkage. Cook bacon on a lower heat, to reduce curling, shrinking and burning. Back and middle rashers should be grilled (broiled) or fried for 2-4 minutes per side, depending on how thick they are. Don't overcook as they can become tough. Streaky bacon should be grilled or fried for 3-6 minutes per side, depending on how crisp you like it. When frying streaky bacon, no additional oil or fat is necessary.

To reduce spatter when frying bacon, fit a wire splatter guard over the pan. To keep bacon slices straight and reduce shrinkage, weigh them down with a metal spatula or fish slice during cooking.

Bacon can also be cooked in the oven. Place the bacon in a single layer in a shallow baking tin or earthenware dish. Bake at 200°C/400°F/Gas 6 for 15-20 minutes or until cooked to your liking. There's no need to turn the bacon as it cooks. Drain on absorbent kitchen paper.

To microwave, place the bacon in a single layer on microwavable kitchen paper on a microwavable plate. Cover with kitchen paper and cook on high to the desired crispness.

Bacon Fat

Adding much flavour, bacon fat keeps food appetizingly succulent and juicy and also fries food to golden crispness.

After cooking bacon, the fat needs to be rendered: strain the fat while it's warm through a coffee filter or kitchen paper into a container, to remove the solid bits left behind after cooking. Store in the refrigerator.

Bacon fat is a culinary staple in America's Deep South where it's known as bacon grease. It's used for frying, to make gravy, to flavour fried greens and roast chicken and drizzled over mashed potatoes and cooked corn.

In Asturias in Spain melted rendered fat is used to enrich stews such as *fabada* (which contains broad beans, chorizo, black-pudding and pork fat) and other meat and savoury dishes.

Strips of fat or fatty bacon can be used to line terrine and pâté moulds and to wrap around poultry or lean cuts of meat during cooking.

The hard fat from the pig's back is also salted or cured like bacon. Translucent white *lardo* is an ancient Italian speciality and every region has its own particular version. The fat is soaked in brine, rubbed with salt, herbs and spices and hung for a few months. Similar products are known in Central and Eastern Europe as *salo*, as *szalonna* in Hungary, *słonina* in Poland and *slanina* in the Czech Republic. In Eastern Europe salo may be salted or brined, whereas in Central Europe it's usually cured with a thick layer of paprika, black pepper or other seasonings; South European salo is more than often smoked.

Above *Strips of streaky bacon are often used to wrap around a terrine to seal in flavour and keep the other ingredients moist.*

Below *Lardo is cured in salt, herbs and spices and is considered a delicacy in Italy.*

BACON COOKING TIPS

• Use kitchen shears to cut bacon into small pieces. Cook until crisp, and add to soups, stews, and salads.

• Adding bacon strips to the breast of a game or poultry bird during roasting keeps the bird moist. Remove the bacon 15 minutes before the end of cooking to ensure an evenly browned surface.

• Keep some cooked bacon to hand to add to sandwiches, burgers, soups and salads.

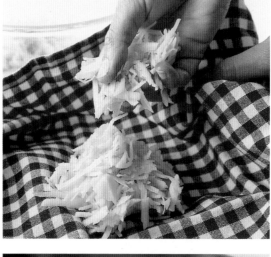

BREAKFASTS

Nothing says bacon more than breakfast, and the traditional British fry-up wouldn't be the same without sizzling rashers alongside the egg and sausage, nor in America a pile of freshly made pancakes and maple syrup without their crispy, salty accompaniment. But there are many other tempting ways to try bacon as well, perfect for a leisurely weekend breakfast or brunch – frazzled bacon or pancetta in a croissant with egg and caviar; bacon griddled in grated potato cakes; and delectable Bacon, Mushroom and Maple Syrup Muffins.

The combination of moreish smoky bacon, lightly poached eggs and Hollandaise sauce on an English muffin has become an American culinary classic.

EGGS BENEDICT

Serves 4

8 slices back bacon
4 eggs
2 English muffins or 4 slices of bread
butter, for spreading
fresh chives, to garnish

For the sauce

3 egg yolks
30ml/2 tbsp fresh lemon juice
1.5ml/¼ tsp salt
115g/4oz/½ cup butter
30ml/2 tbsp single (light) cream
ground black pepper

Energy 553kcal/2304kJ; Protein 19.8g; Carbohydrate 31.6g, of which sugars 2.2g; Fat 39.7g, of which saturates 18.9g; Cholesterol 427mg; Calcium 148mg; Fibre 1.3g; Sodium 635mg.

1 Grill (broil) the bacon slices, set aside and keep warm.

2 To make the sauce, blend the egg yolks, lemon juice and salt in a food processor or blender for 15 seconds. Melt the butter in a small pan until it bubbles. With the motor running, slowly pour the hot butter into the food processor or blender through the feeder tube in a slow, steady stream. Turn off the machine as soon as all the butter has been added.

3 Pour the sauce into a bowl, placed over a pan of simmering water. Stir for 2–3 minutes, until thickened. If the sauce begins to curdle, whisk in 15ml/1 tbsp boiling water. Stir in the cream and season with pepper. Remove from the heat and keep warm over the pan.

4 Bring a shallow pan of water to the boil. Break each egg into the water, turning the white around the yolk with a spoon. Cook for 3–4 minutes. Remove the eggs using a slotted spoon, and drain on kitchen paper.

5 While the eggs are poaching, split and toast the muffins or the slices of bread. Spread with butter while still warm. Place a bacon slice on each muffin or slice of toast, then place an egg on each bacon-topped muffin. Spoon the warm sauce over the eggs, garnish with chives and serve.

Another classic American breakfast, these small, thick, buttery pancakes will be eaten in seconds, so make plenty. The batter can be made the night before.

AMERICAN PANCAKES WITH GRILLED BACON

Serves 4

8 slices back bacon
175g/6oz/1½ cups plain (all-purpose)
  flour, sifted
pinch of salt
15ml/1 tbsp caster (superfine) sugar
2 large eggs
150ml/¼ pint/⅔ cup milk
5ml/1 tsp bicarbonate of soda
  (baking soda)
10ml/2 tsp cream of tartar
oil, for cooking
butter
maple syrup

Energy 324kcal/1358kJ; Protein 12.9g;
Carbohydrate 33g, of which sugars 11.5g; Fat
16.5g, of which saturates 3.5g; Cholesterol
30mg; Calcium 79mg; Fibre 0.9g; Sodium
1153mg.

1 Grill (broil) the bacon slices, set aside and keep warm.

2 To make the batter, mix together the flour, salt and sugar. In a separate bowl, beat the eggs and milk together, then gradually stir into the flour, beating to a smooth, thick consistency. Add the bicarbonate of soda and cream of tartar, mix well, then cover and chill until ready to cook.

3 When you are ready to cook the pancakes, beat the batter again. Heat a little oil in a heavy-based frying pan or griddle. Drop dessertspoonfuls of the mixture into the pan, spaced well apart, and cook over a fairly high heat until bubbles appear on the surface of the pancakes and the undersides become golden brown.

4 Carefully turn the pancakes over with a metal spatula or slice and cook briefly until golden underneath, then transfer them to a heated serving dish. Top each pancake with a little butter and drizzle with maple syrup. Serve the pancakes piled high with 2 slices of grilled bacon.

The enduring popularity of a hearty cooked breakfast depends on using the best ingredients – top-quality sausages, black pudding, and first-class dry-cured bacon

THE GREAT BRITISH FRY-UP

Serves 4

4 lamb's kidneys, halved and trimmed
wholegrain mustard, for spreading
8 slices back or streaky (fatty) bacon,
　preferably dry-cured
275g/10oz black pudding (blood
　sausage), sliced
225g/8oz sausages
butter or oil, for grilling (broiling) or
　frying
4 tomatoes, halved
4–8 flat field (portobello)
　mushrooms
4 potato cakes or potato bread
4 eggs
sea salt and ground black pepper
hot buttered toast, to serve

1 Spread the kidneys with a little mustard. Grill (broil) or fry the bacon, black pudding, kidneys and sausages with butter or oil, as preferred, until crisp and nicely browned. Season to taste, and then keep warm.

2 Meanwhile, fry or grill the halved tomatoes with knobs (pats) of butter, and fry or bake the flat field mushrooms, preferably in the juices from the bacon, kidneys and sausages, until they are just tender.

3 Fry the potato cakes or potato bread until warmed through and golden brown on both sides. Fry the eggs to your liking. Arrange everything on large, warm plates, and serve at once with hot buttered toast.

Energy 894Kcal/3728kJ; Protein 50.6g; Carbohydrate 40.1g, of which sugars 5.5g; Fat 60.4g, of which saturates 20.1g; Cholesterol 618mg; Calcium 115mg; Fibre 3.5g; Sodium 2.25mg

These oaty pancakes have a special affinity with bacon, making an interesting alternative to the big traditional fry-up. Serve with sausages, tomatoes and egg.

OATMEAL PANCAKES WITH BACON

Serves 4

8 slices back bacon
115g/4oz/1 cup fine wholemeal (whole-wheat) flour
25g/1oz/¼ cup fine pinhead oatmeal
pinch of salt
2 eggs
about 300ml/½ pint/1¼ cups buttermilk
butter or oil, for greasing

1 Fry the bacon slices, set aside and keep warm.

2 Mix the flour, oatmeal and salt in a bowl or food processor, beat in the eggs and add enough buttermilk to make a creamy batter of the same consistency as ordinary pancakes.

3 Thoroughly heat a griddle or cast-iron frying pan over a medium-hot heat. When very hot, grease the pan lightly with butter or oil. Pour in a small amount of the batter, about a ladleful at a time. Tilt the pan around to spread evenly and cook for about 2 minutes on the first side, or until set and the underside is browned. Turn over and cook for a further minute until browned.

4 Keep the pancakes warm while you cook the others. Roll the pancakes with a cooked slice of bacon and serve.

Energy 202Kcal/845kJ; Protein 11.9g;
Carbohydrate 13.1g, of which sugars 2g; Fat
11.8g, of which saturates 4.8g; Cholesterol 87mg;
Calcium 59mg; Fibre 1.5g; Sodium 654mg

This delicious American sandwich is a masterpiece of crisp bacon, lettuce, tomato and mayonnaise. Use top-quality dry cured-bacon for the perfect result.

CLASSIC BLT

Makes 2

4 slices granary bread
15 g/½oz/1 tbsp softened butter
few crisp lettuce leaves, cos or
    iceberg
1 large tomato, sliced
8 slices streaky (fatty) bacon
30 ml/2 tbsp mayonnaise

1 Spread 2 of the slices of bread with butter. Lay the lettuce over the bread and cover with sliced tomato.

2 Grill (broil) the bacon until it begins to crisp, then arrange it over the lettuce and sliced tomato.

3 Spread the 2 remaining slices of bread with mayonnaise. Lay over the bacon, press the sandwich together gently and cut in half.

Cook's Tip
As a variation from the classic BLT, add 10ml/2 tsp Dijon mustard to the mayonnaise, and slice an avocado for the filling.

Energy 647kcal/2699kJ; Protein 28g;
Carbohydrate 44g, of which sugars 4g; Fat 41g,
of which saturates 14g; Cholesterol 99mg;
Calcium 198mg; Fibre 6g; Sodium 1941mg.

This breakfast consists of grated potatoes, onion, eggs and chopped bacon shaped into cakes and cooked in tasty bacon fat. Serve with cooked sausages and eggs.

BACON POTATO CAKES

Serves 4–6

250g/9oz potatoes, weighed after
  peeling
1 large onion
175g/6oz rindless streaky (fatty)
  bacon, finely chopped
50g/2oz/½ cup self-raising (self-rising)
  flour
2 eggs
bacon fat or oil, for frying
salt and ground black pepper

1 Grate the potatoes onto a clean dish cloth, and then gather up the edges to make a pouch. Squeeze and twist the towel to remove the liquid.

2 Grate or finely chop the onion into a mixing bowl and add the potatoes, chopped bacon, flour and seasoning, mixing well.

3 Beat the eggs and stir into the potato mixture. Heat some oil in a large frying pan. Add generous tablespoonfuls of the potato mixture to the hot oil and flatten them to make thin cakes. Cook over a medium heat for 3–4 minutes on each side or until golden brown and cooked through. Lift out, drain on kitchen paper and serve.

Energy 214kcal/891kJ; Protein 8.8g; Carbohydrate 17.1g, of which sugars 3.5g; Fat 12.7g, of which saturates 3.4g; Cholesterol 82mg; Calcium 38mg; Fibre 1.4g; Sodium 397mg.

Cook's Tip
Fry the cakes in oiled metal rings if you wish, for a neater circular shape.

A classic combination of eggs, buttery croissants, caviar and crisply fried pancetta, which adds a crunchy smokiness. The ultimate luxury breakfast.

CROISSANTS WITH SCRAMBLED EGGS, CAVIAR AND PANCETTA

Serves 4

4 croissants
50g/2oz/¼ cup butter
12 slices thin smoked pancetta or
    streaky (fatty) bacon
8 free-range (farm-fresh) eggs, at
    room temperature
60ml/4 tbsp crème fraîche
60ml/4 tbsp Avruga or Keta caviar
45ml/3 tbsp chopped fresh chives
salt and ground black pepper

Energy 668kcal/2860kJ; Protein 27g;
Carbohydrate 31g, of which sugars 5g; Fat 51g,
of which saturates 25g; Cholesterol 578mg;
Calcium 88mg; Fibre 2g; Sodium 1297mg.

1 Preheat the oven to 200°C/400°F/Gas 6. Place the croissants on a baking tray and warm them in the oven for about 5 minutes, then switch the oven off.

2 Melt the butter in a non-stick frying pan until foaming, then add the pancetta or bacon. Cook over a high heat until very crisp. Lift out on to a plate and keep warm in the oven with the croissants. Leave the butter and fat in the pan and reheat gently.

3 Lightly beat the eggs with the crème fraîche and season with salt and pepper. Split the croissants in half and place on warmed plates. Pour the eggs into the pan and stir with a wooden spoon. Cook over a low heat, stirring slowly, until the mixture is creamy and thick. Remove the pan from the heat.

4 Fill the croissants with the scrambled eggs, spoon over the caviar and lay the pancetta on top. Sprinkle with chopped chives and serve immediately.

The texture and flavour of crisply fried bacon is perfectly complemented by the earthy chanterelle mushrooms in this rather sophisticated breakfast roll.

BACON, EGG AND CHANTERELLE ROLLS

Serves 4

8 slices back bacon
50g/2oz/4 tbsp unsalted butter, plus
   extra for spreading
115g/4oz/1½ cups chanterelle
   mushrooms, trimmed and halved
60ml/4 tbsp sunflower oil
4 eggs
4 large baps or rolls, split
salt and ground black pepper

Energy 555kcal/2319kJ; Protein 27g;
Carbohydrate 36g, of which sugars 2g; Fat 35g,
of which saturates 16g; Cholesterol 336mg;
Calcium 175mg; Fibre 4g; Sodium 1527mg.

1 Place the bacon in a large non-stick frying pan and fry in its own fat until crisp. Transfer to a heatproof plate, cover and keep warm in a low oven.

2 Melt 25g/1oz/2 tbsp of the butter in the pan, add the chanterelles and fry over a gentle heat until soft, without letting them colour. Transfer to a plate, cover and keep warm.

3 Melt the remaining butter, add the oil and heat to a moderate temperature. Break the eggs into the pan, 2 at a time, if necessary. Fry them, turning to cook both sides if you like.

4 Toast the rolls, spread with butter, then top each with 2 bacon slices, chanterelles and a fried egg. Season, add the roll lids and serve at once.

The strong flavours of bacon and fresh dates are a terrific combination. With the addition of brie, these little muffins are delicious and unusual. The batter will make 12–14 standard muffins, if you prefer.

BACON, BRIE AND FRESH DATE MUFFINS

1 Preheat the oven to 180°C/350°F/Gas 5. Lightly grease the cups of a mini muffin tin (pan) or line them with mini paper cases.

2 In a large bowl, sift together the flour, salt, baking powder and sugar and set aside.

3 Using a knife dusted with flour, chop the dates into small pieces. Separate out any small clumps and add to the flour mixture.

4 In a frying pan, heat the oil and butter over a medium heat, and fry the bacon until crisp, 4 minutes.

5 When it is cool enough to handle, cut the warm bacon into small pieces and stir the pieces back into the warm juices in the pan. Cover with foil and set aside.

6 Mash the brie as finely as you can into the milk, then mix it into the dry ingredients along with the melted butter, eggs, the fried bacon and any juices from the pan. Mix lightly together until just combined.

7 Fill the prepared paper cases three-quarters full. Bake for 18–20 minutes, until risen and golden.

8 Leave to stand and set for 5 minutes before turning out on to a wire rack. Serve warm, or store for up to 3 days in an airtight container.

Makes 24–28 mini muffins

225g/8oz/2 cups plain (all-purpose) flour
pinch of salt
10ml/2 tsp baking powder
10ml/2 tsp caster (superfine) sugar
12 fresh dates, pitted
30ml/2 tbsp olive oil, for frying
15g/½oz/1 tbsp butter, for frying
12 slices smoked streaky (fatty) bacon
75g/3oz brie, diced
150ml/¼ pint/⅔ cup milk
50g/2oz/¼ cup butter, melted
2 eggs, beaten

Energy 183kcal/724kJ; Protein 4.9g; Carbohydrate 12.2g, of which sugars 0.6g; Fat 11.9.6g, of which saturates 8.3g; Cholesterol 53mg; Calcium 99mg; Fibre 0.8g; Sodium 202mg.

These scrumptious muffins make the perfect treat on Sunday morning. A wonderful fusion of sweet, salty-hot and crispy bacon, mushrooms and a drizzle of warm maple syrup for a special occasion brunch.

BACON, MUSHROOM AND MAPLE SYRUP MUFFINS

Makes 8–9 large muffins

225g/8oz/2 cups plain (all-purpose) flour
12.5ml/2½ tsp baking powder
30ml/2 tbsp olive oil, for frying
100g/4oz/8 tbsp butter, for frying
150g/5oz smoked streaky (fatty) bacon
115g/4oz/1½ cups small flat mushrooms, thinly sliced
2 eggs
200ml/7fl oz/scant 1 cup buttermilk
10ml/2 tsp maple syrup
extra slices of streaky (fatty) bacon and maple syrup, to serve

Energy 286kcal/1197kJ; Protein 7.5g; Carbohydrate 29.4g, of which sugars 10.3g; Fat 16.3g, of which saturates 8g; Cholesterol 78mg; Calcium 74mg; Fibre 0.9g; Sodium 399mg.

1 Preheat the oven to 180°C/350°F/Gas 5. Lightly grease the cups of a muffin tin (pan).

2 In a large bowl, sift together the flour and baking powder.

3 In a pan, heat the oil and 25g/1oz/2 tbsp butter and fry the bacon gently until crisp, about 4 minutes. Remove from the heat. Cut into small strips, cover with foil and keep warm.

4 Return the pan to the heat and stir the mushrooms in the hot oil for 30 seconds. Set them aside in the pan.

5 In a small bowl, beat the eggs, buttermilk and 75g/3oz/6 tbsp melted butter together. Pour the liquid into the dry ingredients with the maple syrup. Stir until partly combined.

6 Add the bacon and mushrooms and any juices from the pan and stir in. Do not overmix.

7 Fill the prepared paper cases and bake for 25 minutes until well risen and firm to the touch. Leave to cool slightly then turn out on to a wire rack to cool. Serve with the extra slices of bacon and maple syrup.

Introducing savoury into sweet is always exciting, especially when the savoury is quite salty. Anyone who has tried fried bacon drizzled with maple syrup will know how good it tastes, and it works really well in these moreish doughnuts.

MAPLE BACON DOUGHNUTS

Makes 12 doughnuts

4 slices streaky (fatty) bacon
225g/8oz/2 cups strong white bread
  flour, plus extra for dusting
7g/¼oz/1½ tsp easy-blend (rapid-rise)
  dried yeast
15ml/1 tbsp caster (superfine) sugar
pinch of salt
65g/2½oz/5 tbsp butter, cubed and
  chilled
1 egg, beaten
120ml/4fl oz/½ cup full-fat (whole)
  milk, lukewarm
12 small squares of baking
  parchment
about 1 litre/1¾ pints/4 cups
  sunflower oil, for frying
100ml/3½fl oz/scant ½ cup maple
  syrup

Energy 210kcal/877kJ; Protein 4.1g;
Carbohydrate 25g, of which sugars 11.3g; Fat
11g, of which saturates 3g; Cholesterol 16mg;
Calcium 37mg; Fibre 0g; Sodium 207mg.

1 Fry the bacon slices until crisp and chop finely. Set aside.

2 Sift the flour together with the yeast, caster sugar and salt into a bowl. Add the butter, and rub into the flour mixture using your fingertips. Add the egg and milk, and knead the mixture until it all comes together.

3 Turn out the dough on to a lightly floured work surface and knead for 10 minutes, or until silky smooth. Roll into a ball and place back into the bowl, cover with clear film (plastic wrap) and leave to rest in a warm place for about 1 hour, or until doubled in size.

4 Roll out the dough on a lightly floured work surface until it is roughly 1cm/½in thick, then, using a doughnut cookie cutter, cut out 12 rings and place each of these on to a baking parchment square. Cover loosely with clear film (plastic wrap) and leave to stand in a warm place for 30 minutes, until slightly risen. Heat the oil in a large, deep pan to 170°C/340°F.

5 Gently lift the doughnuts using the edges of the baking parchment, without disturbing the doughnuts, and slide each one (minus the baking parchment) into the hot oil in batches of 3. Cook them for 30–60 seconds on each side, or until golden brown all over. Remove the doughnuts from the oil with a slotted spoon and drain on kitchen paper.

6 For the topping, drizzle the maple syrup over the tops of the doughnuts, while still slightly warm, and brush to coat evenly. Sprinkle with the chopped pieces of bacon.

STARTERS AND LIGHT MEALS

Bacon makes a dish as the main event but also comes into its own as a supporting ingredient, adding an extra dimension with its irresistible salty, smoky or sweet-cured flavours. There's something in this chapter to satisfy everyone, from hearty country soups and delicious quiches and pies to sophisticated starters to whet the appetite, as well as tempting party bites. A little bacon can go a long way, transforming plainer ingredients for a quick and easy pasta supper, and many recipes can be prepared well ahead so are ready to serve when you're short of time.

A hearty meal in a soup bowl. The bacon hock contributes flavour to this dish, but it may be salty so remember to taste and add extra salt only if required.

BACON BROTH

Serves 6

1 bacon hock, about 900g/2lb
75g/3oz/⅓ cup pearl barley
75g/3oz/⅓ cup lentils
2 leeks, sliced, or onions, diced
4 carrots, diced
200g/7oz swede (rutabaga), diced
3 potatoes, diced
small bunch of herbs (thyme, parsley, bay leaf)
1 small cabbage, trimmed, quartered or sliced
salt and ground black pepper
chopped fresh parsley, to garnish

Energy 306Kcal/1284kJ; Protein 17.7g; Carbohydrate 33.5g, of which sugars 8.3g; Fat 12.1g, of which saturates 4.3g; Cholesterol 35mg; Calcium 74mg; Fibre 4.6g; Sodium 1.05g

1 Soak the bacon hock in cold water overnight. Next morning, drain it and put it into a large pan with enough fresh cold water to cover it. Bring to the boil, skim off any scum that rises to the surface, and then add the barley and lentils. Bring back to the boil and simmer for about 15 minutes.

2 Add the leeks, carrots and swede to the pan with some black pepper and the herbs. Bring back to the boil, reduce the heat and simmer gently for 1½ hours, or until the meat is tender.

3 Lift the bacon hock from the pan with a slotted spoon. Remove the skin, then take the meat off the bones and break it into bitesize pieces. Return to the pan with the cabbage. Discard the herbs and cook for a little longer until the cabbage is cooked to your liking.

4 Adjust the seasoning and ladle into large serving bowls, garnish with parsley and serve with freshly baked brown bread.

Cook's tip Traditionally, the cabbage is simply trimmed and quartered, although it may be sliced if you prefer.

This thick and warming split pea soup makes a substantial starter, or it may be served as a meal in its own right, eaten with hot crusty bread.

BACON, PEA AND BARLEY SOUP

Serves 6

225g/8oz/1¼ cups yellow split peas
25g/1oz/¼ cup pearl barley
1.75 litres/3 pints/7½ cups vegetable
  or ham stock
50g/2oz smoked streaky (fatty)
  bacon, cubed
25g/1oz/2 tbsp butter
1 onion, finely chopped
2 garlic cloves, crushed
225g/8oz celeriac, cubed
15ml/1 tbsp chopped fresh
  marjoram
salt and ground black pepper

Energy 209kcal/882kJ; Protein 11g; Carbohydrate 28g, of which sugars 2g; Fat 7g, of which saturates 3g; Cholesterol 14mg; Calcium 22mg; Fibre 4.6g; Sodium 635mg.

1 Rinse the peas and barley in a sieve under cold running water. Put in a bowl, cover with plenty of water and leave to soak overnight.

2 The next day, drain and rinse the peas and barley. Put them in a large pan, pour in the stock and bring to the boil. Turn down the heat and simmer gently for 40 minutes.

3 Dry-fry the bacon cubes in a frying pan for 5 minutes, or until well browned and crispy. Remove with a slotted spoon, leaving the fat behind, and set aside.

4 Add the butter to the frying pan, add the onion and garlic and cook gently for 5 minutes. Add the celeriac and cook for a further 5 minutes, or until the onion is just starting to colour.

5 Add the softened vegetables and bacon to the pan of stock, peas and barley. Season lightly with salt and pepper, then cover and simmer for 20 minutes, or until the soup is thick. Stir in the marjoram, add extra black pepper to taste and serve with bread.

The strong flavour of smoked bacon pairs beautifully with the mellowness of celeriac and makes an excellent soup. It tastes very good topped with a complementary seasonal version of a salsa.

CELERIAC SOUP WITH CABBAGE, BACON AND HERBS

Serves 4

50g/2oz butter
2 onions, chopped
675g/1½lb celeriac, roughly diced
450g/1lb potatoes, roughly diced
1.2 litres/2 pints/5 cups vegetable
  stock
150ml/¼ pint/⅔ cup single (light)
  cream
salt and ground black pepper
sprigs of fresh thyme, to garnish

For the cabbage and bacon topping

1 small savoy cabbage
50g/2oz/¼ cup butter
175g/6oz rindless streaky (fatty)
  bacon, roughly chopped
15ml/1 tbsp chopped fresh thyme
15ml/1 tbsp chopped fresh rosemary

1 Melt the butter in a saucepan. Add the onions and cook for 4–5 minutes, until softened. Add the celeriac. Cover the vegetables with a wetted piece of greaseproof (waxed) paper, then put a lid on the pan and cook gently for 10 minutes.

2 Remove the paper and stir in the potatoes and stock. Bring to the boil, reduce the heat and simmer for 20 minutes or until the vegetables are very tender. Leave to cool slightly. Using a draining spoon, remove about half the celeriac and potatoes from the soup and set them aside.

3 Purée the soup in a food processor or blender. Return the soup to the rinsed-out pan with the reserved celeriac and potatoes.

4 Prepare the cabbage and bacon mixture. Discard the tough outer leaves from the cabbage. Roughly tear the remaining leaves, discarding any hard stalks, and blanch them in boiling salted water for 2–3 minutes. Refresh under cold running water and drain.

5 Melt the butter in a large frying pan and cook the bacon for 3–4 minutes. Add the cabbage, thyme and rosemary, and stir-fry for a further 5–6 minutes, until tender. Season well.

6 Add the cream to the soup and season it well, then reheat gently until piping hot. Ladle the soup into bowls and pile the cabbage mixture in the centre of each portion. Garnish with sprigs of fresh thyme.

Energy 462kcal/1919kJ; Protein 12.3g; Carbohydrate 24.3g, of which sugars 7.3g; Fat 35.8g, of which saturates 20.4g; Cholesterol 97mg; Calcium 144mg; Fibre 4.3g; Sodium 954mg.

Pickled cabbage, sauerkraut, is very common all over Eastern and Central Europe. In this tasty recipe, the sauerkraut and barley absorb all the flavour and fat from the bacon to produce an intense soup.

SAUERKRAUT AND SMOKED BACON SOUP

Serves 6

10g/¼oz/½ tbsp butter
1 onion, chopped
200g/7oz smoked bacon, cubed
30ml/2 tbsp barley
500g/1¼ lb sauerkraut, chopped
7.5ml/1½ tsp sweet paprika
3–4 sage leaves finely sliced
60ml/4 tbsp sour cream
salt and ground black pepper

1 Melt the butter in a large pan over medium heat and add the onion and bacon. Cook gently for 2–3 minutes,

2 Add the barley and sauerkraut and mix to combine with the onion and bacon. Then cook for 5 minutes, stirring well.

3 Sprinkle with the paprika and add 1.5 litres/2½ pints/6¼ cups water, then bring to the boil.

4 Simmer over medium heat for 20–30 minutes, stirring occasionally. Adjust the seasoning. Serve the thick soup with sage leaves on top and a spoonful of the sour cream.

Variations
• To create a meatier soup, add smoked hocks or a ham bone.
• You can use roux or potatoes to thicken the soup instead of barley.

Energy 155kcal/643kJ; Protein 9g; Carbohydrate 8g, of which sugars 3g; Fat 10g, of which saturates 5g; Cholesterol 33mg; Calcium 62mg; Fibre 0.7g; Sodium 1086mg

Bacon-wrapped oysters served on hot buttered toast are a British classic that dates back to the 19th century, in an era when oysters were plentiful and cheap. The strong flavours go together perfectly and nowadays this little dish makes a delicious starter or finger food for a special party.

ANGELS ON HORSEBACK

Serves 4

16 oysters, removed from their shells
fresh lemon juice
8 slices rindless streaky (fatty) bacon
8 small slices of bread
butter, for spreading
paprika (optional)

Energy 326kcal/1365kJ; Protein 20.3g;
Carbohydrate 26.4g, of which sugars 1.4g; Fat
16.2g, of which saturates 6.9g; Cholesterol 79mg;
Calcium 147mg; Fibre 0.8g; Sodium 1483mg

1 Preheat the oven to 200°C/400°F/Gas 6. Sprinkle the oysters with a little lemon juice.

2 Lay the bacon on a board, slide the back of a knife along each one to stretch it and then cut it in half crosswise. Wrap a piece of bacon around each oyster and secure with a wooden cocktail stick (toothpick). Arrange them on a baking sheet.

3 Put the oysters and bacon into the hot oven for 8–10 minutes until the bacon is just cooked through.

4 Meanwhile, toast the bread. When the bacon is cooked, butter the hot toast and serve the bacon-wrapped oysters on top. Sprinkle with a little paprika, if using.

A popular savoury of bacon-wrapped prunes, this makes an enjoyable appetizer. The prunes are sometimes filled with pâté, olives, almonds or nuggets of cured meat. The delectable combination of luscious sweet prunes and crisp salty bacon is sensational. They can also be served on hot buttered toast, if preferred.

DEVILS ON HORSEBACK

Serves 4

16 stoned prunes
fruit chutney, such as mango
8 slices rindless streaky (fatty) bacon
8 small slices of bread
butter for spreading

Energy 309kcal/1303kJ; Protein 14.7g; Carbohydrate 41.7g, of which sugars 18.3g; Fat 10.4g, of which saturates 3.5g; Cholesterol 30mg; Calcium 75mg; Fibre 3.6g; Sodium 1132mg

1 Preheat the oven to 200°C/400°F/Gas 6. Ease open the prunes and spoon a small amount of fruit chutney into each cavity .

2 Lay the bacon on a board, slide the back of a knife along each one to stretch it and then cut in half crosswise. Wrap a piece of bacon around each prune and lay them close together (if they touch each other, they are less likely to unroll during cooking) on a baking sheet.

3 Put into the hot oven for 8–10 minutes until the bacon is thoroughly cooked through.

4 Meanwhile, toast the bread. Butter the hot toast and serve the bacon-wrapped prunes on top.

In northern Vietnam, beef often features on the street menu. Wrapping the beef in bacon keeps it juicy and has the bonus of adding flavour. If you use smoked bacon, the smokiness will enhance the experience even more.

BACON-WRAPPED BEEF ON SKEWERS

1 To make the marinade, mix all the marinade ingredients in a large bowl until the sugar dissolves. Season generously with black pepper. Add the beef strips, coating them in the marinade, and set aside for about an hour.

2 Preheat a griddle pan over a high heat. Roll up each strip of beef and wrap it in a slice of bacon. Thread the rolls on to the skewers, so that you have 3 on each one.

3 Cook the bacon-wrapped rolls for 4–5 minutes, turning once, until the bacon is golden and crispy. Serve immediately, with *nuoc cham* for dipping.

Cook's Tips
• To prevent the wooden skewers from burning on the griddle, soak them in water for 24 hours
• Nuoc cham is a Vietnamese sweet and sour dipping sauce generally made from fish sauce, chilli, lime juice and sugar. It can be found in many Asian delicatessens.

Serves 4

225g/8oz beef fillet or rump, cut
  across the grain into 12 strips
12 thin slices streaky (fatty) bacon
4 bamboo skewers, soaked in water
nuoc cham, for dipping

For the marinade
15ml/1 tbsp groundnut (peanut) oil
30ml/2 tbsp *nuoc cham*
30ml/2 tbsp soy sauce
4–6 garlic cloves, crushed
10ml/2 tsp sugar
ground black pepper

Per portion Energy 279Kcal/1155kJ; Protein 21.7g; Carbohydrate 1.0g, of which sugars 1.0g; Fat 21.3g, of which saturates 7.1g; Cholesterol 69mg; Calcium 6mg; Fibre 0g; Sodium 750mg

Rillettes is a type of rustic pâté. This version made with pork, bacon and herbs is a celebration of the pig! It makes a great starter, delicious snack or light meal.

PORK AND BACON RILLETTES

Serves 8

1.8kg/4lb belly of pork, boned and cut into cubes (reserve the bones)
450g/1lb rindless streaky (fatty) bacon, finely chopped
5ml/1 tsp salt
1.5ml/¼ tsp ground black pepper
4 garlic cloves, finely chopped
2 fresh parsley sprigs
1 bay leaf
2 fresh thyme sprigs
1 fresh sage sprig
300ml/10fl oz/1¼ cups water

For the onion salad

1 small red onion, halved and finely sliced
2 spring onions (scallions), cut into matchstick strips
2 celery sticks, cut into matchstick strips
15ml/1 tbsp freshly squeezed lemon juice
15ml/1 tbsp light olive oil
ground black pepper

1 In a large bowl, mix the pork, bacon and salt. Cover and leave at room temperature for 30 minutes. Preheat the oven to 150°C/300°F/Gas 2. Stir the pepper and garlic into the meat. Tie the herbs together to make a bouquet garni and mix this into the meat.

2 Spread the meat mixture in a large roasting tin and pour in the water. Place the bones from the pork on top and cover tightly with foil. Cook for 3½ hours.

3 Discard the bones and herbs, and ladle the meat mixture into a metal sieve set over a large bowl. Allow the liquid to drain through into the bowl, then turn the meat into a shallow dish. Repeat until all the meat is drained. Reserve the liquid. Use two forks to pull the meat apart into fine shreds.

4 Line a 1.5 litre/2½ pint/6¼ cup terrine or deep, straight-sided dish with clear film (plastic wrap) and spoon the shredded meat into it. Strain the reserved liquid through a sieve lined with muslin (cheesecloth) and pour it over the meat. Leave to cool. Cover and chill in the refrigerator for at least 24 hours, or until the rillettes has set.

5 To make the onion salad, place the sliced onion, spring onions and celery in a bowl. Add the freshly squeezed lemon juice and light olive oil and toss gently. Season with a little freshly ground black pepper, but do not add any salt as the rillettes is well salted.

6 Serve the rillettes, cut into thick slices, on individual plates with a little onion salad and thick slices of crusty French bread.

Cook's Tip

Ask the butcher to bone and chop the pork and to let you have the bones because they contribute an excellent flavour to the rillettes.

Energy 347kcal/1443kJ; Protein 2g; Carbohydrate 1g, of which sugars 27g; Fat 27g, of which saturates 9g; Cholesterol 87mg; Calcium 23mg; Fibre 1g; Sodium 688mg.

Laver bread (cooked Welsh seaweed) and bacon is a traditional time-honoured Welsh pairing. The meaty bacon is the perfect match for the distinctive salty flavour of the seaweed, but if you prefer, you can use boiled spinach instead.

LAVER BREAD AND BACON OMELETTE

Makes 1 omelette

1 slice lean back bacon, cooked and
  cubed
oil, to prepare the pan
3 eggs
10ml/2 tsp butter
25g/1oz prepared laver bread
salt and ground black pepper

Energy 355kcal/1472kJ; Protein 23.6g;
Carbohydrate 0.5g, of which sugars 0.4g; Fat 29.2g,
of which saturates 11.4g; Cholesterol 605mg;
Calcium 131mg; Fibre 0.5g; Sodium 691mg.

1 Fry the bacon until just crisp, and cut into strips. Set aside and keep warm.

2 Heat a little oil in an omelette pan then leave for a few minutes to help season the pan. A non-stick or small curved-sided pan may also be used.

3 Break the eggs into a bowl large enough for whisking, season then whisk until the yolk and white are well combined but not frothy.

4 Pour the oil out of the pan and reheat. Add the butter, which should begin to sizzle straight away. If it does not the pan is too cool, or if it burns it is too hot. Rinse out, dry and try again.

5 Pour the whisked eggs into the pan and immediately, using the back of a fork, draw the mixture towards the middle of the pan, working from the outside and using quick circular movements going around the pan.

6 As it is beginning to cook but is not quite set, put the bacon and laver bread evenly over one half of the omelette. Cook for another 30 seconds then remove from the heat. Fold one side of the mixture over the side with the bacon and laver bread, leave for a minute or two, then turn out on to a warmed plate. Serve immediately while piping hot.

Crisp on the outside, soft and tender inside, these traditional Swiss potato cakes are a national favourite and taste even better with the addition of bacon.

BACON AND HERB RÖSTI

Serves 4

450g/1lb potatoes, left whole and unpeeled
30ml/2 tbsp olive oil
1 red onion, finely chopped
4 slices rindless lean back bacon, cubed
15ml/1 tbsp potato flour
30ml/2 tbsp chopped fresh mixed herbs
salt and ground black pepper
fresh parsley sprigs, to garnish

Energy 245kcals/1025kJ; Fat, total 12.6g; saturated fat 2.9g; Protein 10.7g; Carbohydrate 23.6g; sugar 1.8g; Fibre 2.6g; Sodium 572mg

1 Lightly grease a baking sheet. Par-boil the potatoes in a pan of lightly salted, boiling water for about 6 minutes. Drain the potatoes and set aside to cool slightly.

2 Once cool enough to handle, peel the potatoes and coarsely grate them into a bowl. Set aside.

3 Heat 15ml/1 tbsp of the oil in a frying pan, add the onion and bacon and cook gently for 5 minutes, stirring occasionally. Preheat the oven to 220°C/425°F/Gas 7.

4 Remove the pan from the heat. Stir the bacon mixture, remaining oil, potato flour, herbs and seasoning into the grated potatoes and mix well.

5 Divide the mixture into 8 small piles and spoon them on to the prepared baking sheet, leaving a little space between them.

6 Bake for 20–25 minutes until the rösti are crisp and golden brown. Serve immediately, garnished with sprigs of fresh parsley.

In this classic open sandwich, the sweet combination of apples and onions mixed with crisp, salty bacon is both rich and satisfying.

APPLE AND BACON OPEN SANDWICH

Serves 4

8 slices unsmoked back bacon
75g/3oz/1 cup finely chopped onion
2 firm apples, peeled and chopped
25g/1oz/2 tbsp salted butter,
  softened
2 slices rye bread
2 leaves round (butterhead) lettuce
fresh parsley sprigs, to garnish

Energy 215kcal/895kJ; Protein 9.8g; Carbohydrate
13.9g, of which sugars 8g; Fat 13.7g,
of which saturates 6.4g; Cholesterol 40mg;
Calcium 21mg; Fibre 2g; Sodium 883mg.

1 Fry the bacon over a medium-high heat until they crispen; drain the bacon on kitchen paper, leaving the fat in the pan.

2 Cook the finely chopped onion in the reserved bacon fat for about 5–7 minutes, until transparent but not browned. Add the chopped apples, and continue cooking for a further 5 minutes, until tender.

3 Crumble half the bacon into the apple mixture.

4 Butter the slices of bread to the edges, top with the lettuce leaves and cut each slice in half. Spoon the apple and bacon mixture on to the lettuce, dividing it evenly among the sandwiches.

5 Break the 4 reserved bacon slices in half, and place 2 pieces on each sandwich. Garnish with parsley sprigs, and serve warm.

Spicy pancetta is a key ingredient of this popular Italian classic pasta dish. Easy to make, it is a satisfying last-minute supper.

SPAGHETTI WITH EGGS, BACON AND CREAM

Serves 4

30ml/2 tbsp olive oil
1 small onion, finely chopped
1 large garlic clove, crushed
8 slices pancetta or rindless smoked streaky (fatty) bacon, cut into 1cm/½in strips
350g/12oz fresh or dried spaghetti
4 eggs
90–120ml/6–8 tbsp/½ cup crème fraîche
60ml/4 tbsp freshly grated Parmesan cheese, plus extra to serve
salt and ground black pepper

Energy 708kcal/2966kj; Protein 30.7g; Carbohydrate 66.6g; of which sugars 4.2g; Fat 37.5g; of which saturates 15.5g; Cholesterol 261mg; Calcium 250mg; Fibre 2.8g; Sodium 824mg.

1 Heat the oil in a large saucepan, add the onion and garlic and fry gently for about 5 minutes until softened. Add the pancetta or bacon to the pan and cook for 10 minutes, stirring.

2 Meanwhile, cook the spaghetti in a large saucepan of salted boiling water according to the instructions on the packet until *al dente*.

3 Put the eggs, crème fraîche and grated Parmesan in a bowl. Stir in plenty of black pepper, then beat together well.

4 Drain the pasta thoroughly, tip it into the pan with the pancetta or bacon mixture and toss well to mix. Turn off the heat under the pan, then immediately add the egg mixture and toss thoroughly.

5 Season to taste, divide the spaghetti among 4 bowls and sprinkle with ground black pepper. Serve, with grated Parmesan handed separately.

The strong flavours of bacon and radicchio are softened with cream in this fabulously tasty Italian dish. It makes an excellent dinner party first course.

TAGLIATELLE WITH BACON AND RADICCHIO

Serves 4

225g/8oz dried tagliatelle
8 slices pancetta or rindless streaky (fatty) bacon, cubed
25g/1oz/2 tbsp butter
1 onion, finely chopped
1 garlic clove, crushed
1 head of radicchio, about 115–175g/4–6oz, finely shredded
150ml/5fl oz/⅔ cup panna da cucina or double (heavy) cream
50g/2oz/⅔ cup freshly grated Parmesan cheese
salt and ground black pepper

Energy 543kcal/2264kJ; Protein 15.7g;
Carbohydrate 44g, of which sugars 3.9g; Fat 35g,
of which saturates 20g; Cholesterol 89mg;
Calcium 197mg; Fibre 2.1g; Sodium 422mg.

1 Cook the pasta according to the instructions on the packet.

2 Meanwhile, put the pancetta or bacon in a medium pan and heat gently until the fat runs. Increase the heat slightly and stir-fry the pancetta or bacon for 5 minutes.

3 Add the butter, onion and garlic to the pan and stir-fry for 5 minutes more. Add the radicchio and toss for 1–2 minutes until wilted.

4 Pour in the cream and add the grated Parmesan, with salt and pepper to taste. Stir for 1–2 minutes until the cream is bubbling and the ingredients are evenly mixed. Taste the sauce for seasoning.

5 Drain the pasta and transfer it into a warmed bowl. Pour the sauce over the pasta and toss well. Serve immediately.

The most famous dumplings in Hungary, these tasty galuska are combined with crisply fried bacon as a light meal. Serve with a green salad, if you like.

NOODLES AND BACON

Serves 6

2 eggs
5ml/1 tsp salt
200ml/7fl oz/scant 1 cup water
about 300g/11oz/2⅔ cups plain
    (all-purpose) flour
45ml/3 tbsp fresh mixed herbs, such
    as parsley, tarragon, thyme and
    rosemary, finely chopped
200g/7oz smoked bacon, cubed
30ml/2 tbsp vegetable oil
salt
melted butter, to serve

Energy 337kcal/1514kJ; Protein 13g;
Carbohydrate 39g, of which sugars 1g; Fat 16g,
of which saturates 5g; Cholesterol 102mg;
Calcium 99mg; Fibre 2.4g; Sodium 626mg

1 Beat the eggs with the salt and water. Add a little flour to make a smooth and thick mixture, then add the remaining flour and beat with a wooden spoon until the dough is glossy and exceptionally smooth.

2 Add the herbs and mix in well. Adjust the dough with more flour, if necessary, until it comes away from the sides of the bowl.

3 Place the dough on a board and, using a teaspoon, cut off noodles about 2.5cm/1in long and to the thickness of a pencil. Add the noodles to a pot of boiling water. Alternatively, push the dough through a dumpling strainer directly into the boiling water. Cook until the galuska rise to the top of the water, then drain them in a colander.

4 Meanwhile, sauté the cubed bacon in a non-stick pan with the vegetable oil until golden and crispy. Serve the hot galuska with some melted butter and topped with the crispy bacon.

This delicious quiche recipe has some very traditional characteristics; namely very thin pastry, a creamy, light egg-rich filling, and appetizing smoked bacon.

QUICHE LORRAINE

Serves 4–6

175g/6oz/1½ cups plain (all-purpose)
   flour, sifted
pinch of salt
115g/4oz/½ cup butter, plus
   25g/1oz/2 tbsp butter, to serve
3 eggs, plus 3 yolks
6 slices smoked rindless streaky
   (fatty) bacon
300ml/10fl oz/1¼ cups double
   (heavy) cream
salt and ground black pepper

Energy 670kcal/2775kJ; Protein 13g;
Carbohydrate 23.7g, of which sugars 1.4g; Fat
58.9g, of which saturates 32.9g; Cholesterol
302mg; Calcium 94mg; Fibre 0.9g; Sodium
611mg.

1 Place the flour, salt, butter and 1 egg yolk in a food processor and process until blended. Tip out on to a lightly floured surface and bring the mixture together into a ball. Leave to rest for 20 minutes.

2 Lightly flour a deep 20cm/8in round flan tin, and place it on a baking tray. Roll out the pastry and use to line the tin, trimming off any overhanging pieces. Gently press the pastry into the corners of the tin. If the pastry breaks up, don't worry, just gently push it into shape. Chill for 20 minutes. Preheat the oven to 200°C/400°F/Gas 6.

3 Meanwhile, cut the bacon into thin strips and grill (broil) until the fat runs. Arrange the bacon in the pastry case. Beat together the cream, the remaining eggs and yolks and seasoning, and pour into the pastry case.

4 Bake for 15 minutes, then reduce the heat to 180°C/350°F/Gas 4 and bake for a further 15–20 minutes. When the filling is puffed up and golden brown and the pastry edge crisp, remove from the oven and top with knobs of butter. Stand for 5 minutes before serving.

Bacon makes these mouthwatering little pies extra tasty and keeps the filling moist. They can be made up to a day ahead of being served and they are a good choice for a summer picnic or special packed lunch.

Makes 12

10ml/2 tsp sunflower oil
1 onion, chopped
225g/8oz pork, coarsely chopped
115g/4oz cooked bacon, finely diced
45ml/3 tbsp chopped mixed fresh
   herbs
6 eggs, hard-boiled and halved
1 egg yolk, beaten
20g/¾ oz packet powdered aspic
300ml/10fl oz/1¼ cups boiling water
salt and ground black pepper

For the hot water crust pastry
450g/1lb/4 cups plain (all-purpose)
   flour
115g/4oz/½ cup white vegetable fat
   or lard
275ml/9fl oz/generous 1 cup water

Energy 311kcal/1302kJ; Protein 12.1g;
Carbohydrate 30.4g, of which sugars 1.6g; Fat
16.4g, of which saturates 5.5g; Cholesterol
135mg; Calcium 77mg; Fibre 1.5g; Sodium 74mg.

MINI PORK AND BACON PIES

1 Preheat the oven to 200°C/400°F/Gas 6. To make the hot water crust pastry, sift the flour into a bowl and add a good pinch each of salt and pepper. Gently heat the fat or lard and water in a large pan until the fat has melted. Increase the heat and bring to the boil.

2 Remove the pan from the heat and pour the liquid into the flour, stirring. Press the mixture into a smooth ball of dough using the back of a spoon – take care as the dough is very hot. When smooth, cover the bowl and set it aside.

3 Heat the oil in a frying pan, add the onion and cook until soft. Stir in the pork and bacon and cook until browning. Remove from the heat and stir in the herbs and seasoning.

4 Roll out two-thirds of the pastry on a lightly floured work surface. Use a 12cm/4½in round cutter to stamp out rounds to line 12 muffin tins. Place a little meat mixture in each pie, then add half an egg to each and top with the remaining meat.

5 Roll out the remaining pastry and use a 7.5cm/3in round cutter to stamp out lids for the pies. Dampen the rims of the pastry bases and press the lids in place. Pinch the edges to seal. Brush with egg yolk and make a small hole in the top of each pie to allow the steam to escape. Bake for 30–35 minutes. Leave to cool for 15 minutes, then transfer to a wire rack to cool completely.

6 Meanwhile, stir the aspic powder into the boiling water until dissolved. Shape a piece of foil into a small funnel and use this to guide a little aspic in through the hole in the top of each pie. Leave them to cool and set, then chill for up to 24 hours before serving.

Whole eggs are broken over richly succulent smoked bacon and softened onions before being covered in pastry in a double-crust pie, in this celebration of simple but fine ingredients. It is perfect for an alfresco lunch or family picnic.

BACON AND EGG PIE

1 To make the pastry, sift the flour and salt into a large bowl and rub or cut in the fat until the mixture resembles fine breadcrumbs. Sprinkle over most of the water and mix to a pliable dough, adding more water if required. Knead until smooth, then wrap in clear film (plastic wrap) and chill for 30 minutes.

2 Butter a deep 20cm/8in flan tin (quiche pan). Roll out two-thirds of the pastry and use to line the flan tin. Cover the pastry case. Chill for approximately 30 minutes.

3 Preheat the oven to 200°C/400°F/Gas 6. Heat the oil in a pan, add the bacon and cook for a few minutes, then add the onion and cook until soft. Drain on kitchen paper and leave to cool.

4 Cover the base of the pastry case with the bacon mixture, spreading it evenly, then break the eggs on to the bacon, spacing them evenly apart. Carefully tilt the flan tin so the egg whites flow together. Sprinkle the eggs with the chopped parsley, a little salt and plenty of black pepper. Place a baking sheet in the oven to heat.

5 Roll out the remaining pastry, dampen the edges and place over the pie. Roll over the top with a rolling pin to seal the edge and remove the excess pastry. With a sharp knife, carefully cut curved lines from the centre of the lid to within 2cm/¾in of the edge. Lightly brush the pie with the milk to glaze.

6 Place the pie on the hot baking sheet and bake for 10 minutes, then lower the oven temperature to 180°C/350°F/Gas 4 and bake for a further 20 minutes. Leave to cool for a few minutes before cutting and serving.

Serves 6

30ml/2 tbsp sunflower oil
4 slices smoked bacon, cut into
    4cm/1½in pieces
1 small onion, finely chopped
5 eggs
25ml/1½ tbsp chopped fresh parsley
salt and ground black pepper
a little milk, to glaze

For the pastry

350g/12oz/3 cups plain (all-purpose)
    flour
pinch of salt
115g/4oz/½ cup butter, diced
50g/2oz/¼ cup lard or white
    vegetable fat
75–90ml/5–6 tbsp chilled water

Energy 202kcal/843kJ; Protein 13.4g; Carbohydrate 9.7g, of which sugars 4.4g; Fat 12.5g, of which saturates 4.2g; Cholesterol 149mg; Calcium 125mg; Fibre 1.1g; Sodium 592mg.

Bacon and leeks are a wonderful flavour combination in this versatile tart. While it makes a deliciously savoury first course, it is equally suitable served in more generous proportions with a mixed leaf salad for a light lunch or supper.

LEEK AND BACON TART

Makes 6–8 individual tartlets

275g/10oz/2½ cups plain (all–purpose) flour
pinch of salt
175g/6oz butter
2 egg yolks
about 45ml/3 tbsp very cold water
green salad leaves, to garnish

For the filling

225g/8oz streaky (fatty) bacon, cubed
4 leeks, sliced
6 eggs
115g/4oz/½ cup cream cheese
15ml/1 tbsp mild mustard
pinch of cayenne pepper
salt and ground black pepper

1 Sieve the flour and salt into a bowl, and rub in the butter until it resembles fine breadcrumbs. Add the egg yolks and just enough water to combine the dough. Alternatively, you can use a food processor. Wrap the dough in clear film (plastic wrap) and place in the refrigerator for approximately 30 minutes.

2 Meanwhile, preheat the oven to 200°C/400°F/Gas 6. Roll out the pastry thinly and use to line 6–8 tartlet cases or a 28cm/11in tart dish. Remove any air pockets and prick the base with a fork. Line the pastry loosely with baking parchment, weigh down with baking beans and bake the pastry shell blind for 15–20 minutes, or until golden.

3 To make the filling, cook the bacon in a hot pan until crisp. Add the leeks and continue to cook for 3–4 minutes until just softening. Remove from the heat. In a bowl, beat the eggs, cream cheese, mustard, cayenne pepper and seasoning together, then add the leeks and bacon.

4 Remove the paper and baking beans from the tartlet or tart case, pour in the filling and bake for 35–40 minutes.

5 To serve, plate the tartlets on to individual serving plates or cut the tart into narrow wedges and serve warm, with a small salad garnish.

Energy 487Kcal/2026kJ; Protein 15.4g; Carbohydrate 28.2g, of which sugars 1.6g; Fat 35.7g, of which saturates 19.1g; Cholesterol 265mg; Calcium 107mg; Fibre 2.1g; Sodium 681mg

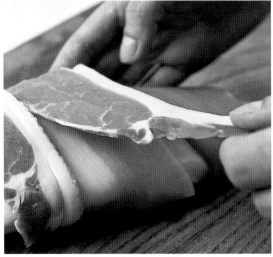

FISH AND SEAFOOD

The combination of bacon with seafood can be a revelation, high-lighting and bringing out the flavour of succulent fish and shellfish without overwhelming it. It works as a wonderful contrast for the sweet juiciness of scallops and white fish, or can hold its own against the strong tastes of smoked haddock or salty herring. The versatile bacon is also used here as tasty wrappings around fish fillets with a crispy breadcrumb stuffing, or around grilled eel chunks infused with lemon grass and ginger.

This is a classic combination: the smokiness of the fish goes well with the rich flavour of the bacon, and both are complemented by the creamy sauce.

SMOKED HADDOCK AND BACON

Serves 4

25g/1oz/2 tbsp butter
4 undyed smoked haddock fillets
8 slices lean back bacon
120ml/4floz/½ cup double
   (heavy) cream
ground black pepper
chopped fresh chives, to garnish

1 Preheat the grill (broiler) to medium. Over a gentle heat, melt the butter in a frying pan.

2 Add the haddock fillets, working in two batches if necessary, and cook gently, turning once, for about 3 minutes each side. When cooked, place in a large ovenproof dish and cover. Reserve the juices from the frying pan.

3 Grill (broil) the bacon, turning once, until just cooked through but not crispy. Leave the grill on.

4 Return the frying pan to the heat and pour in the cream and any reserved juices from the haddock. Bring to the boil then simmer briefly, stirring occasionally. Season to taste with ground black pepper.

5 Meanwhile place 2 bacon rashers over each haddock fillet and place the dish under the grill (broiler) briefly. Then pour over the hot creamy sauce, garnish with snipped fresh chives and serve immediately.

Variation

This dish is equally delicious with the addition of wilted spinach. Thoroughly wash a good handful of spinach for each person. Then plunge it into boiling water for 3 minutes, drain well and lay across each fillet interspersed with the bacon strips.

Energy 391kcal/1624kJ; Protein 28.8g; Carbohydrate 0.5g, of which sugars 0.5g; Fat 30.5g, of which saturates 16.5g; Cholesterol 119mg; Calcium 40mg; Fibre 0g; Sodium 1671mg.

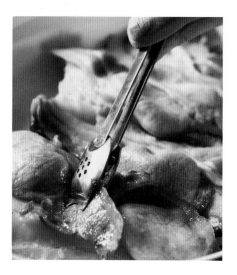

Scallops and bacon are a traditional pairing in Scottish and English cooking. The streaky bacon perfectly balances the sweetness of the scallops.

Serves 4 as a starter or 2 as a main course

15ml/1 tbsp olive oil

4 slices streaky (fatty) bacon, cut into 2.5cm/1in strips

2–3 fresh sage leaves, chopped

small piece of butter

8 large or 16 small scallops

15ml/1 tbsp fresh lemon juice

100ml/3½fl oz/scant ½ cup dry cider or white wine

lemon wedges, to serve

Energy 179kcal/745kJ; Protein 15.6g; Carbohydrate 1.9g, of which sugars 0.2g; Fat 10.4g, of which saturates 3.3g; Cholesterol 42mg; Calcium 19mg; Fibre 0g; Sodium 414mg

SCALLOPS WITH BACON AND SAGE

1 Heat a frying pan and add the oil, bacon and sage. Gently cook, stirring occasionally, until the bacon is golden brown. Lift out and keep warm.

2 Add the butter to the pan and when hot add the scallops. Cook for about 1 minute on each side until browned. Lift out and keep warm with the bacon.

3 Add the lemon juice and cider to the pan and, scraping up any sediment, bring just to the boil. Continue bubbling gently until the mixture has reduced to a few tablespoons of syrupy sauce.

4 Serve the scallops and bacon with the sauce drizzled over, and a freshly sliced lemon wedge.

This recipe uses the classic combination of scallops with bacon, but this time using princess scallops which are cooked with flavoursome cured bacon.

PRINCESS SCALLOPS WITH SMOKED BACON

Serves 4

6 slices smoked streaky (fatty) bacon, cut into thin strips
5ml/1 tsp ground turmeric
28 princess scallops
1 sprig each of parsley and thyme
1 bay leaf
6 black peppercorns
150ml/5fl oz/⅔ cup dry white wine
75ml/2½fl oz/⅓ cup double (heavy) cream
30ml/2 tbsp chopped fresh chives, to garnish

Energy 353kcal/1476kJ; Protein 36.5g; Carbohydrate 4.8g, of which sugars 0.5g; Fat 18.4g, of which saturates 9.1g; Cholesterol 106mg; Calcium 51mg; Fibre 0g; Sodium 904mg.

1 Using a pan with a close-fitting lid, fry the bacon in its own fat until well cooked and crisp. Remove the bacon.

2 Reduce the heat to low, stir the turmeric into the juices and cook for 1–2 minutes.

3 Add the scallops to the pan with the herbs and peppercorns. Carefully pour in the wine (it will steam) and then cover with the lid. The scallops will only take a few minutes to cook. Test them by removing a thick one and piercing with a sharp knife to see if it is soft. Once they are cooked, remove from the pan and keep warm.

4 Stir in the cream and increase the heat to allow the sauce to simmer. This should be a light sauce; if it becomes too thick then add a little water.

5 Serve the scallops in warmed bowls or on plates with the sauce ladled over. Sprinkle with the crisp bacon and garnish with chopped fresh chives.

Smoked bacon in a nutty stuffing is the perfect foil for rich smoky mackerel. In this recipe, mackerel are stuffed, tied with raffia and then grilled (broiled). They taste just as good cold so, when mackerel are at their peak, make extra for lunch the next day and serve with horseradish mayonnaise and some peppery rocket.

RAFFIA-TIED MACKEREL WITH NUTTY BACON STUFFING

Serves 6

45ml/3 tbsp olive oil
2 onions, finely chopped
2 garlic cloves, crushed
6 slices rindless smoked bacon, cubed
50g/2oz/½ cup pine nuts
45ml/3 tbsp chopped fresh sweet marjoram
6 mackerel, about 300g/11oz each, cleaned but with heads left on
salt and ground black pepper
lemon wedges, to serve
raffia, soaked in water

1 Heat the oil in a large frying pan and sweat the chopped onions and garlic over a medium heat for 5 minutes. Increase the heat and add the bacon and pine nuts. Fry for a further 5–7 minutes, stirring occasionally, until golden. Tip into a bowl to cool. Gently fold in the sweet marjoram, season lightly, cover and chill until needed.

2 To prepare each fish, snip the backbone at the head end. Extend the cavity opening at the tail end so you can reach the backbone more easily. Turn the fish over and, with the heel of your hand, press firmly along the entire length of the backbone to loosen it. Snip the bone at the tail end and it will lift out surprisingly easily. Season the insides lightly.

3 Stuff the cavity in each mackerel with some of the chilled onion mixture, then tie the mackerel along its entire length with raffia to hold in the stuffing. Chill the fish for at least 15 minutes. They can be chilled for up to 2 hours, but if so, allow them to come to room temperature for about 15 minutes before grilling.

4 Prepare the barbecue. Once the flames have died down, position a lightly oiled grill rack over the coals to heat. When the coals are medium-hot, or with a moderate coating of ash, transfer the mackerel to the grill rack and cook for about 8 minutes on each side, or until cooked and golden. If your barbecue has a lid, use it. This will help you achieve an even golden skin without needing to move the fish about. Serve the mackerel with lemon wedges and black pepper.

Cook's Tip
If you are cooking these on a charcoal kettle barbecue, and the heat is too intense, reduce it a little by half-closing the air vents.

Energy 645kcal/2674kJ; Protein 44g; Carbohydrate 4g, of which sugars 3g; Fat 50g, of which saturates 10g; Cholesterol 125mg; Calcium 37mg; Fibre 1g; Sodium 494mg.

Wrapping trout in fatty bacon helps to retain moisture and adds flavour, particularly to farmed fish. If you are lucky enough to obtain wild trout you will appreciate just how well its earthy flavour works with the bacon and leek. Make sure you use dry-cure bacon for this traditional dish.

TROUT WITH BACON

1 Preheat the oven to 180°C/350°F/Gas 4. Rinse the trout, inside and out, under cold running water, then pat dry with kitchen paper. Season the cavities and put a few parsley sprigs and a slice of lemon into each.

2 Wrap 2 leek leaves, then 2 bacon rashers, spiral-fashion around each fish. It may be helpful to secure the ends of the bacon with wooden cocktail sticks (toothpicks).

3 Lay the fish in a shallow ovenproof dish, in a single layer and side by side, head next to tail.

4 Bake for about 20 minutes, until the bacon is cooked and the leeks are tender. The trout should be cooked through; check by inserting a sharp knife into the thickest part.

5 Sprinkle the remaining parsley over the trout and serve.

Cook's Tips
• This dish is nicer to eat if the backbone is removed from the fish first – ask your fishmonger to do this. Leave the head and tail on or cut them off, as you prefer.
• Use tender leaves (layers) of leek, rather than the tough outer ones. Alternatively, soften some leaves by pouring boiling water over them and leaving them to stand for a few minutes before draining.

Serves 4

4 trout, each weighing about 225g/8oz, cleaned
small parsley sprigs
4 lemon slices plus lemon wedges to serve
8 large leek leaves
8 slices rindless back bacon
salt and ground black pepper

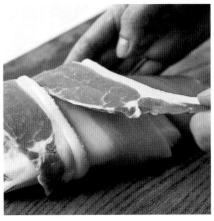

Energy 324kcal/1357kJ; Protein 44.4g; Carbohydrate 0.4g, of which sugars 0.3g; Fat 16.1g, of which saturates 5.1g; Cholesterol 174mg; Calcium 60mg; Fibre 0.3g; Sodium 997mg

The combination of crisp bacon and flaky white fish is always good and the bacon keeps the fish moist and tender as it cooks. Serve with boiled new potatoes and steamed green seasonal vegetables.

STUFFED WHITE FISH WRAPPED IN BACON

Serves 4

4 good-size or 8 small fish fillets, such as whiting, trimmed
4 slices streaky (fatty) bacon

For the stuffing

50g/2oz/¼ cup butter
1 onion, finely chopped
50g/2oz/1 cup fine fresh brown breadcrumbs
5ml/1 tsp finely chopped fresh parsley
good pinch of mixed dried herbs
sea salt and ground black pepper

1 Preheat the oven to 190°C/375°F/Gas 5. Trim the fish fillets. If they are fairly big, cut them in half lengthways; leave small ones whole. Remove the rind and any gristle from the streaky bacon slices.

2 To make the stuffing, melt the butter in a small pan, add the onion and cook gently until softened but not browned. Add the breadcrumbs, parsley and herbs. Season to taste.

3 Divide the stuffing between the fillets, roll them up and wrap a bacon slice around each one.

4 Secure the rolls with wooden cocktail sticks (toothpicks) and lay them in a single layer in the base of a shallow buttered baking dish. Cover with foil and bake in the preheated oven for 15 minutes, removing the cover for the last 5 minutes. Serve with potatoes and green beans if liked.

Energy 344Kcal/1436kJ; Protein 38.1g; Carbohydrate 12.5g, of which sugars 2.4g; Fat 15.9g, of which saturates 8.2g; Cholesterol 120mg; Calcium 44mg; Fibre 0.8g; Sodium 662mg

Flavoursome chopped bacon and tender matjes herring are the focal flavours of this easy-to-make salad. If you find the salty herring taste too strong, soak the fillets in milk for a couple of hours before cooking.

MATJES HERRING WITH BACON AND ONIONS

1 Boil the potatoes in salted water until tender. Meanwhile, cook the trimmed beans in boiling salted water for 6–8 minutes, then drain and refresh under cold running water. They should still be crisp with a fresh green colour.

2 Heat the butter in a pan over medium heat and fry the bacon in it for about 3 minutes, then add the chopped onion. Cook for a further minute, then add the cooked beans. Season with salt and pepper and stir in the chopped savory.

3 Drain the potatoes and arrange on a serving plate with the herring fillets and the beans. Garnish with onion rings.

Cook's Tips
• If you can't find savory, use some fresh thyme instead.
• Sauce remoulade, or tartare sauce, makes a good accompaniment for this dish.

Serves 4

1kg/2¼lb potatoes, peeled
1kg/2¼lb green beans, trimmed
100g/3½oz butter
200g/7oz thickly sliced streaky (fatty) bacon, diced
3 onions, 2 chopped and 1 sliced into fine rings
8 matjes herring fillets
15ml/1 tbsp chopped fresh savory
salt and ground white pepper

Energy 970kcal/4032kJ; Protein 47.4g; Carbohydrate 58.1g, of which sugars 16g; Fat 53.4g, of which saturates 26.1g; Cholesterol 203mg; Calcium 199mg; Fibre 9.8g; Sodium 1103mg

Crisp, streaky bacon works well with the rich, oily texture of firm-fleshed eel. This Asian recipe is best served with a dipping sauce, a crunchy salad, and jasmine rice.

GRILLED EEL WRAPPED IN BACON WITH LEMON GRASS AND GINGER

Serves 4–6

2 lemon grass stalks, trimmed and chopped
25g/1oz fresh root ginger, peeled and chopped
2 garlic cloves, chopped
2 shallots, chopped
15ml/1 tbsp palm sugar
15ml/1 tbsp vegetable or groundnut (peanut) oil
30ml/2 tbsp *nuoc mam* or *tuk trey*
1.2kg/2½lb fresh eel, skinned and cut into 2.5cm/1in pieces
12 slices streaky (fatty) bacon
freshly ground black pepper
a small bunch of fresh coriander (cilantro) leaves, to garnish
nuoc cham, for dipping

1 Using a mortar and pestle, pound the lemon grass, ginger, garlic and shallots with the sugar to form a paste. Add the oil and *nuoc mam* or *tuk trey*, mix well and season with black pepper. Put the eel pieces in a dish and smear them thoroughly in this paste. Cover and place in the refrigerator for 2–3 hours to marinate.

2 Wrap each piece of marinated eel in a strip of bacon, gathering up as much of the marinade as possible.

3 To cook the eel parcels, you can use a conventional grill (broiler), a well-oiled griddle pan, or a barbecue. If grilling over charcoal, you can skewer the eel parcels; otherwise, spread them over the grill or griddle pan. Cook the eel parcels until nice and crispy, roughly 2–3 minutes on each side. Serve with fresh coriander leaves and *nuoc cham* for dipping.

Cook's Tip
When buying fresh eel, it's worth asking the fishmonger to gut it, cut off the head, bone it, skin it and slice it for you – it makes life easier!

Energy 460Kcal/1911kJ; Protein 39.3g;
Carbohydrate 0.8g, of which sugars 0.6g; Fat
33.3g, of which saturates 9g; Cholesterol 324mg;
Calcium 43mg; Fibre 0.1g; Sodium 650mg

MEAT AND POULTRY

There are classic main-course bacon recipes here such as Loin of Bacon with Cabbage and Parsley Sauce, or Bacon Chops with Apple and Cider Sauce. But bacon also provides the magic ingredient that can transform a roast chicken from the everyday to the special, bring richly flavoured undertones to a Coq au Vin, and lift a herby stuffing for roast partridge. A classic sun-dried tomato risotto is given depth with the addition of smoky bacon, and a simple but moreish Potato and Bacon Bake is sure to become a stand-by supper dish.

Adding chopped smoked bacon is the perfect finishing touch to this satisfying dish of succulent roast chicken and pears.

ROAST CHICKEN WITH BACON AND PEARS

1 First, make the accompaniments. Peel the pears, but leave them whole. Remove the calyx from the base, but leave the stalks. Place them in a heavy pan with the vanilla pod and sugar, add water almost to cover and bring to the boil. Lower the heat, cover and simmer for 1 hour. Add the wine, re-cover the pan and simmer for a further 2 hours.

2 Using a slotted spoon, transfer the pears to a wide dish, standing them upright. Measure 500ml/17fl oz/generous 2 cups of the cooking liquid, pour into a clean pan and bring to the boil.

3 Mix the potato flour with 90ml/6 tbsp cold water to a paste in a bowl and stir into the cooking liquid. Cook, stirring, until the liquid starts to thicken, then remove from the heat. Pour the sauce over the pears and set aside to cool.

4 Stuff the chicken with 1 peeled, whole onion and the lemon balm. Rub the outside with salt and pepper. Place the chicken in an ovenproof casserole pot, cover with the lid and place in the cold oven. Set the temperature to 240°C/475°F/Gas 9 and cook for 30 minutes.

5 Meanwhile, chop the remaining onion and season the potato slices. Remove the pot from the oven and arrange the potato slices around the chicken. Sprinkle the diced bacon and chopped onion on top.

6 Cover the pot and return to the oven for 45 minutes. Remove the lid from the pot and cook the chicken for a further 5–10 minutes, until evenly browned.

7 Garnish with lemon balm leaves and serve the chicken straight from the pot, handing the pears around separately.

Serves 4

1.2kg/2½lb free-range (barnyard) chicken
2 onions
a large bunch of lemon balm, plus extra leaves to garnish
800g/1¾lb waxy potatoes, sliced
100g/3¾oz/scant ⅔ cup diced lean smoked bacon
salt and pepper

For the pears

1kg/2¼lb red cooking pears
½ vanilla pod (bean)
45ml/3 tbsp sugar
dash of red wine
45ml/3 tbsp potato flour

Energy 829kcal/3466kJ; Protein 47.4g; Carbohydrate 79.2g, of which sugars 40.2g; Fat 37.3g, of which saturates 11.1g; Cholesterol 213mg; Calcium 69mg; Fibre 7.9g; Sodium 573mg.

Old-fashioned suet puddings are still a favourite, and this one is filled with a tasty filling of unsmoked bacon, tender chickens and leeks. Serve it with seasonal vegetables or a green salad tossed lightly in an oil and vinegar dressing.

Serves 4

200g/7oz unsmoked lean, rindless bacon, preferably in one piece
400g/14oz skinless boneless chicken, preferably thigh meat
2 small or medium leeks, finely chopped
30ml/2 tbsp finely chopped fresh parsley
175g/6oz/1¼ cups self-raising (self-rising) flour
75g/3oz/½ cup shredded suet
120ml/4fl oz chicken or vegetable stock, or water
ground black pepper
butter for greasing

BACON, CHICKEN AND LEEK PUDDING

1 Cut the bacon and chicken into bitesize pieces into a large bowl. Mix them with the leeks and half the parsley. Season with black pepper.

2 Sift the flour into another large bowl and stir in the suet and the remaining parsley. With a round-bladed knife, stir in sufficient cold water to make a soft dough. On a lightly floured surface, roll out the dough to a circle measuring about 33cm/13in across. Cut out one quarter of the circle (starting from the centre, like a wedge), roll up and reserve.

3 Lightly butter a 1.2 litre/2 pint pudding bowl. Use the rolled-out dough to line the buttered bowl, pressing the cut edges together to seal them and allowing the pastry to overlap the top of the bowl slightly.

4 Spoon the bacon and chicken mixture into the lined bowl, packing it neatly and taking care not to split the pastry. Pour the chicken or vegetable stock over the bacon mixture, making sure it does not overfill the bowl.

5 Roll out the reserved pastry into a circle to form a lid and lay it over the filling, pinching the edges together to seal them well. Cover with baking parchment (pleated in the centre to allow the pudding to rise) and then a large sheet of foil (again pleated at the centre). Tuck the edges under and press them tightly to the sides of the bowl until well sealed.

6 Steam the pudding over boiling water for about 3½ hours. Check the water level occasionally. Uncover the pudding, slide a knife around the sides and turn out on to a warmed serving plate.

Per portion Energy 535kcal/2236kJ; Protein 28.2g; Carbohydrate 39.4g, of which sugars 2.9g; Fat 31.3g, of which saturates 14.8g; Cholesterol 86mg; Calcium 111mg; Fibre 4g; Sodium 999mg

The bacon helps to 'baste' the chicken while it cooks and brings out the delicious taste of roast chicken as well as the aromatic stuffing. Quinoa is an excellent gluten-free stuffing ingredient to use instead of breadcrumbs. If used in place of sausagemeat it also lowers the fat content.

LEMON AND QUINOA-STUFFED ROAST CHICKEN

1 Heat the oven to 200°C/400°F/Gas 6. Prepare the stuffing. Heat the oil in a pan and add the garlic, onion, quinoa and water. Bring to the boil, and simmer for 12–14 minutes, until the quinoa is soft to bite. Drain off any excess water. Mix in the remaining stuffing ingredients and season.

2 Loosely stuff the neck cavity of the chicken two-thirds full; heat must be able to circulate inside the bird. Weigh the stuffed chicken and calculate the cooking time based on 20 minutes per 450g/1lb plus 10–20 minutes, and then 30 minutes resting time.

3 Brush the outside of the chicken with olive oil, season with salt and pepper and cover with the slices of bacon. Place in the hot oven for 20 minutes, then baste with the juices and reduce the temperature to 190°C/375°F/Gas 5.

4 Par-boil the root vegetables for about 3 minutes in a covered pan. Drain, add the quinoa flour, parsley and seasoning. Toss to coat and set aside.

5 About 20 minutes before the end of the chicken's cooking time, place the olive oil for the roast vegetables in an ovenproof casserole and heat. Remove the bacon from the chicken, set aside, and baste the chicken.

6 Add the quinoa-coated vegetables to the hot casserole, turning to coat in the oil, then place in the oven.

7 When the chicken is cooked, test by inserting a skewer into the thickest part of the thigh and checking that the juices run clear, remove from the oven and set aside, covered, to rest.

8 Increase the oven temperature to 200°C/400°F/Gas 6 and roast the vegetables for 15 minutes, until crispy.

9 Carve the chicken and serve with the crispy bacon, a spoonful of stuffing and the quinoa-coated roast vegetables.

Serves 4

1 x 1.3kg/3lb whole free-range (barnyard) chicken
15ml/1 tbsp olive oil
4 slices streaky (fatty) bacon
salt and ground black pepper

For the stuffing

15ml/1 tbsp vegetable oil
2 cloves garlic, crushed
1 medium onion, finely chopped
125g/4¼oz/¾ cup pearl quinoa
475ml/16fl oz/2 cups water
2 lemons, juice of both, grated rind of 1
25g/1oz/¼ cup quinoa flour
25g/1oz fresh sage, finely chopped
25g/1oz capers, roughly chopped
25g/1oz butter
salt and ground black pepper

For the roast vegetables

600g/1lb 6oz mixed root vegetables (beetroot (beet), swede (rutabaga), sweet potato, parsnip, celeriac), peeled and cut into 4cm/1½in batons
25g/1oz/¼ cup quinoa flour
15ml/1 tbsp chopped fresh parsley
30ml/2 tbsp olive oil
salt and ground black pepper

Energy 778kcal/3257kJ; Protein 56g; Carbohydrate 50g, of which sugars 12g; Fat 41g, of which saturates 11g; Cholesterol 186mg; Calcium 161mg; Fibre 8g; Sodium 878mg.

A simple but impressive dish that is both sweet and tangy, and enlivened by the rich savoury smoked bacon sauce.

CHICKEN IN SMOKY BACON SAUCE

Serves 4

2 large whole free-range (barnyard) chickens
25g/1oz/2 tbsp butter
10ml/2 tsp sunflower oil
115g/4oz smoked streaky (fatty) bacon, chopped
2 leeks, washed and sliced
175g/6oz/2¼ cup small button (white) mushrooms, trimmed
120ml/4fl oz/½ cup apple juice, plus a further 15ml/1 tbsp
120ml/4fl oz/½ cup chicken stock
30ml/2 tbsp clear honey
10ml/2 tsp chopped fresh thyme or 2.5ml/½ tsp dried
225g/8oz crisp red apples
10ml/2 tsp cornflour (cornstarch)
salt and ground black pepper

Energy 465Kcal/1945kJ; Protein 32.8g; Carbohydrate 25.9g, of which sugars 20.7g; Fat 26.3g, of which saturates 9.5g; Cholesterol 172mg; Calcium 40mg; Fibre 3.3g; Sodium 632mg.

1 Using a sharp, heavy knife or a meat cleaver, carefully split the chickens in half to make 4 portions. Rinse the portions well under cold running water, then pat dry using kitchen paper.

2 Heat the butter and sunflower oil in a large pan and add the chicken portions. Fry, turning the pieces over, until lightly browned on all sides. Transfer the chicken portions to a large casserole dish, leaving the cooking fat in the pan.

3 Add the chopped bacon to the pan and cook for about 5 minutes, stirring occasionally, until beginning to brown. Using a slotted spoon transfer the bacon to the casserole dish, leaving all the juices behind.

4 Add the leeks and mushrooms to the pan and cook for a few minutes until they begin to soften and the mushrooms begin to release their juices.

5 Pour 120ml/4fl oz/½ cup apple juice and the chicken stock into the pan, then stir in the honey and thyme. Season well.

6 Bring the mixture almost to boiling point, then pour over the chicken and bacon. Cover the casserole dish with the lid and cook for 1 hour over a medium heat.

7 Quarter, core and thickly slice the apples. Add them to the cooking pot, submerging them in the liquid to stop them turning brown. Cook for a further 30 minutes, or until the chicken and vegetables are cooked and tender. Remove the chicken from the cooking pot, place on a plate and keep warm.

8 Blend the cornflour with the 15ml/1 tbsp apple juice and stir into the cooking liquid until thickened. Taste and adjust the seasoning, if necessary.

9 Serve the chicken on warmed plates with sauce poured over the top. Accompany with mashed potatoes and pan-fried or steamed baby leeks, if liked.

Strips of fat or fatty bacon ensure that the lean gamey partridge stays moist and succulent and prevents the flesh from drying out as it cooks. It is important that you choose young birds for this recipe.

ROAST PARTRIDGES WITH BACON, HERBS AND GARLIC

1 Preheat the oven to 190°C/375°F/Gas 5. Season the partridges well inside and out, then place in a roasting pan.

2 Lay the slices of bacon over the birds.

3 Mix together the softened butter, herbs and garlic, and use to stuff the cavities of the birds.

4 Place in the oven and roast for about 1½ hours, until cooked through, basting often with the extra butter.

5 Remove from the oven, cover with foil and allow to rest for 15 minutes.

6 Serve with cranberry preserve, if you like.

Cook's Tip
To test if the partridges are cooked, pierce the thickest part of the thigh; the juices should run clear.

Serves 4

4 small partridges, cleaned and gutted
8 slices streaky (fatty) bacon
50g/2oz/¼ cup butter, softened, plus 45ml/3 tbsp melted butter, for basting
10 fresh sage leaves, roughly chopped
1 bunch fresh thyme, leaves chopped
10 garlic cloves, roughly chopped
salt and ground black pepper, to taste
cranberry preserve, to serve (optional)

Energy 866kcal/3619kJ; Protein 118g; Carbohydrate 0.1g, of which sugars 0.1g; Fat 43.6g, of which saturates 16.1g; Cholesterol 59mg; Calcium 145mg; Fibre 0g; Sodium 1006mg.

Chopped smoked bacon really rounds out the flavour of this mouthwatering classic French casserole. Serve with boiled potatoes, if you like.

COQ AU VIN

Serves 6

45ml/3 tbsp light olive oil
12 shallots
225g/8oz streaky (fatty) bacon, chopped
3 garlic cloves, finely chopped
225g/8oz small mushrooms, halved
6 boneless chicken thighs
3 boneless chicken breasts, halved
1 bottle red wine
salt and ground black pepper
45ml/3 tbsp chopped fresh parsley, to garnish

For the bouquet garni

3 sprigs each of fresh parsley, thyme and sage
1 bay leaf and 4 peppercorns

For the beurre manié

25g/1oz/2 tbsp butter, softened
25g/1oz/¼ cup plain (all-purpose) flour

Energy 474kcal/1977kJ; Protein 35g; Carbohydrate 5g, of which sugars 1g; Fat 26g, of which saturates 8g; Cholesterol 146mg; Calcium 35mg; Fibre 1g; Sodium 563mg.

1 Heat the oil in a large, flameproof casserole and cook the shallots for 5 minutes, or until golden. Increase the heat, add the bacon, garlic and mushrooms and cook for a further 10 minutes, stirring frequently.

2 Use a draining spoon to transfer the cooked ingredients to a plate, then brown the chicken portions in the oil remaining in the pan, turning them until they are golden brown all over. Return the shallots, garlic, mushrooms and bacon to the casserole and pour in the red wine.

3 Tie the ingredients for the bouquet garni in a bundle in a small piece of muslin (cheesecloth) and add to the casserole. Bring to the boil, reduce the heat and cover the casserole, then simmer for 30–40 minutes.

4 To make the beurre manié, cream the butter and flour together in a small bowl to make a smooth paste.

5 Add small lumps of this paste to the bubbling casserole, stirring well until each piece has melted into the liquid before adding the next. When all the paste has been added, bring back to the boil and simmer for 5 minutes.

6 Season the casserole to taste with salt and pepper and serve garnished with the chopped fresh parsley and accompanied by boiled potatoes.

Simple, yet packed with flavour, this is a quick and easy economical meal. Serve with creamy mashed potatoes to soak up the sauce and lightly steamed greens, if you like. Don't overcook the liver, as it will only toughen.

LIVER, BACON AND ONIONS

1 Pat the liver with kitchen paper, then trim it and, with a sharp knife, cut on the diagonal to make thick strips. Season the flour and toss the liver in it until well coated, shaking off any excess flour.

2 Heat the oil in a large frying pan and add the bacon. Cook over medium heat until the fat runs out of the bacon and it is browned and crisp. Lift out and keep warm.

3 Add the onions and sage to the frying pan. Cook over medium heat for about 10–15 minutes, stirring occasionally, until the onions are soft and golden brown. Lift out with a draining spoon and keep warm.

4 Increase the heat under the pan and, adding a little extra oil if necessary, add the liver in a single layer. Cook for 3–4 minutes, turning once, until browned both sides.

5 Return the onions to the pan and pour in the stock. Bring just to the boil and bubble gently for a minute or two, seasoning to taste with salt and pepper. Serve topped with the bacon.

Serves 4

450g/1lb lamb's liver
30ml/2 tbsp plain (all-purpose) flour
15ml/1 tbsp oil, plus extra if
  necessary
8 slices rindless streaky (fatty) bacon
2 onions, thinly sliced
4 fresh small sage leaves, finely
  chopped
150ml/5fl oz/⅔ cup chicken or
  vegetable stock
salt and ground black pepper

Energy 310kcal/1293kJ; Protein 28.7g;
Carbohydrate 13.7g, of which sugars 5.7g; Fat
15.9g, of which saturates 4.4g; Cholesterol
500mg; Calcium 44mg; Fibre 1.6g; Sodium 400mg

This traditional Irish dish, reputedly a favourite of Jonathan Swift, combines bacon and sausages, two foods used throughout Ireland's culinary history.

POTATO, BACON AND SAUSAGE CASEROLE

Makes 4 large or 8 small portions

8 thick dry-cured bacon slices
8 best-quality lean pork sausages
4 large onions, thinly sliced
900g/2lb potatoes, sliced
90ml/6 tbsp chopped fresh parsley
salt and ground black pepper

Energy 432Kcal/1809kJ; Protein 20.6g;
Carbohydrate 52g, of which sugars 10.2g; Fat
17.2g, of which saturates 6.1g; Cholesterol 45mg;
Calcium 83mg; Fibre 5.7g; Sodium 1.27g

1 Cut the bacon into large strips and cook with the sausages in 1.2 litres/ 2 pints/5 cups boiling water for 5 minutes. Drain the bacon, but reserve the cooking liquor.

2 Put the meat into a pan or ovenproof dish with the onions, potatoes and the parsley. Season, and add just enough of the reserved cooking liquor to cover. Cover with a tight-fitting lid; lay a piece of buttered foil or baking parchment on top before putting on the lid.

3 Simmer gently over a low heat for about 1 hour, or until the liquid is reduced by half and all the ingredients are cooked but not mushy. Serve hot with the vegetables on top, with the traditional accompaniments of fresh soda bread, steamed greens, and a glass of stout, if you like.

Full-flavoured meaty bacon chops marry beautifully with the tangy apple and mustard sauce. Serve with mashed potatoes and steamed buttered cabbage.

BACON CHOPS WITH APPLE AND CIDER SAUCE

Serves 4

15ml/1 tbsp oil
4 bacon chops
1 or 2 cooking apples
knob (pat) of butter
1 or 2 garlic cloves, finely chopped
5ml/1 tsp sugar
150ml/5fl oz/⅔ cup dry (hard) cider
5ml/1 tsp cider vinegar
15ml/1 tbsp wholegrain mustard
10ml/2 tsp chopped fresh thyme
salt and ground black pepper
sprigs of thyme, to garnish

Energy 285Kcal/1190kJ; Protein 26.4g;
Carbohydrate 6.5g, of which sugars 6.5g; Fat
16.1g, of which saturates 5.4g; Cholesterol 40mg;
Calcium 17mg; Fibre 0.8g; Sodium 1.34g

1 Heat the oil in a large heavy frying pan, over a medium heat, and cook the chops for 10–15 minutes, browning well on both sides.

2 Peel, core and slice the apples. Remove the chops from the pan and keep warm. Add the butter and apples to the pan and cook until the juices begin to brown.

3 Add the finely chopped garlic and sugar, and cook for 1 minute, then stir in the cider, cider vinegar, mustard and chopped thyme. Boil for a few minutes until reduced to a saucy consistency.

4 Season to taste and place the chops on warmed serving plates. Garnish with the thyme sprigs and serve.

The Eastern European answer to fast food is a meat loaf, prepared using a mixture of good-quality veal or beef and pork. This recipe uses smoked ham or bacon to wrap the loaf. Serve sliced with boiled new potatoes, if you like.

MEAT LOAF

1 Preheat the oven to 180°C/350°F/ Gas 4 and grease a 20–25cm/8–10in loaf tin. Put the milk in a bowl and add the bread slices. Leave to soak for a few minutes then squeeze out the excess liquid.

2 Bring a small pan of water to the boil and cook 4 eggs for 7 minutes. Remove and leave to cool completely.

3 Put the soaked bread in a large bowl, add the onion, beef, pork, thyme and parsley. Beat the remaining egg and add to the bowl. Season with salt and pepper. Combine the mixture well.

4 Line the loaf tin with bacon slices, leaving enough hanging over the edges for wrapping around the loaf.

5 Fill the tin with the meat mixture. Peel the eggs and gently press into the loaf, along its full length, burying the eggs into the centre.

6 Wrap the bacon around the meat loaf. Place the tin on a baking tray. Bake for 1 hour, or until the loaf is golden brown. Serve hot or cold.

Serves 6

100ml/3½fl oz/scant ½ cup milk
2 slices of white bread
5 large (US extra large) eggs
1 large onion, grated
350g/12oz/1½ cups minced (ground) beef
350g/12oz/1½ cups minced (ground) pork
leaves from 1 small bunch fresh thyme
½ bunch of parsley leaves, chopped
12 slices smoked rindless streaky (fatty) bacon
salt and ground black pepper

Energy 401kcal/1673kJ; Protein 33.1g; Carbohydrate 11.3g, of which sugars 5g; Fat 25.4g, of which saturates 9.3g; Cholesterol 250mg; Calcium 102mg; Fibre 1.5g; Sodium 476mg.

Bacon loin is the focal point of this modern interpretation of an old favourite and brings together a number of classic ingredients. Traditional accompaniments include boiled or mashed potatoes or mashed swede.

LOIN OF BACON WITH CABBAGE AND PARSLEY SAUCE

Serves 6

1.3kg/3lb loin of bacon
1 carrot, chopped
2 celery sticks, chopped
2 leeks, chopped
5ml/1 tsp peppercorns
15ml/1 tbsp wholegrain mustard
15ml/1 tbsp oven-dried breadcrumbs
7.5ml/1½ tsp light muscovado
    (brown) sugar
25g/1oz/2 tbsp butter
900g/2lb green cabbage, sliced

For the parsley sauce
50g/2oz/¼ cup butter
25g/1oz/¼ cup plain (all-purpose)
    flour
150ml/5fl oz/⅔ cup single (light)
    cream
bunch of parsley, leaves chopped
salt and ground black pepper

Energy 689Kcal/2857kJ; Protein 40.4g;
Carbohydrate 16.3g, of which sugars 10.6g; Fat
51.5g, of which saturates 23.1g; Cholesterol
155mg; Calcium 139mg; Fibre 5g; Sodium 3.46g

1 Place the bacon joint in a large pan. Add the vegetables to the pan, with the peppercorns. Cover with cold water and bring to the boil. Simmer gently for about 20 minutes per 450g/1lb. Preheat the oven to 200°C/400°F/Gas 6.

2 Remove the joint from the pan, reserving 150ml/¼ pint/⅔ cup of the cooking liquid. Remove the rind, and score the fat. Place the joint in a roasting pan. Mix the mustard, breadcrumbs, sugar and 15g/½oz/1 tbsp butter; spread this mixture evenly over the joint. Cook in the oven for 15–20 minutes.

3 To make the parsley sauce, melt the butter in a small pan, then add the flour and cook for 1–2 minutes, stirring constantly. Whisk in the cooking liquid and cream. Bring to the boil. Reduce the heat and simmer for 3–4 minutes, then stir in the chopped fresh parsley. Season to taste. The sauce should have the consistency of thin cream. Set aside and keep warm.

4 In another pan cook the cabbage with a little of the cooking liquid from the bacon. Drain well, season to taste and toss in the remaining butter.

5 To serve, slice the bacon and serve on a bed of cabbage, with a little of the parsley sauce.

A classic comforting risotto, with plenty of onions, smoked bacon and sun-dried tomatoes. You'll want to keep going back for more.

RISOTTO WITH SMOKED BACON AND TOMATO

1 Drain the sun-dried tomatoes and reserve 15ml/1 tbsp of the oil. Chop the tomatoes and set aside. Cut the bacon into 2.5cm/1in pieces.

2 Heat the oil from the sun-dried tomatoes in a large saucepan. Fry the bacon until well cooked and golden. Remove with a slotted spoon and drain on kitchen paper.

3 Heat 25g/1oz/2 tbsp of the butter in a saucepan and fry the onions and garlic over a medium heat for 10 minutes, until soft and golden brown.

4 Stir in the rice. Cook for 1 minute, until the grains turn translucent. Stir the wine into the stock. Add a ladleful of the mixture to the rice and cook gently until the liquid has been absorbed.

5 Stir in another ladleful of the stock and wine mixture and allow it to be absorbed. Repeat this process until all the liquid has been used up. This should take 25–30 minutes. The risotto will turn thick and creamy, and the rice should be tender but not sticky.

6 Just before serving, stir in the bacon, sun-dried tomatoes, Parmesan, half the herbs and the remaining butter. Adjust the seasoning (remember that the bacon is quite salty) and serve sprinkled with the remaining herbs.

Serves 4–6

8 sun-dried tomatoes in olive oil
275g/10oz rindless smoked back
  bacon
75g/3oz/6 tbsp butter
450g/1lb onions, roughly chopped
2 garlic cloves, crushed
350g/12oz/1¾ cups risotto rice
300ml/10fl oz/1¼ cups dry white
  wine
1 litre/1¾ pints/4 cups simmering
  vegetable stock
50g/2oz/⅔ cup freshly grated
  Parmesan cheese
45ml/3 tbsp mixed chopped fresh
  chives and flat leaf parsley
salt and ground black pepper

Energy 513kcal/2133kJ; Protein 16.9g; Carbohydrate 55.1g, of which sugars 6.8g; Fat 21.3g, of which saturates 11.1g; Cholesterol 59mg; Calcium 159mg; Fibre 2.1g; Sodium 885mg.

Bacon provides lots of flavour in this recipe, one of the most famous in Lithuania, where it is called kugelis. The version here is less fatty than the Lithuanian original. It is often served topped with crispy onion rings.

POTATO AND BACON BAKE

Serves 6

800g/1¾lb potatoes, peeled and grated
2 eggs, beaten
30ml/2 tbsp potato flour
2.5ml/½ tsp baking powder
200g/7oz smoked bacon, cubed
2 shallots, finely chopped
2.5ml/½ tsp caraway seeds, ground
30ml/2 tbsp finely chopped fresh dill
salt and ground black pepper

For the onion rings

100ml/3½fl oz/scant ½ cup vegetable oil
1 large onion, sliced into rings
30ml/2 tbsp plain (all-purpose) flour

Energy 211kcal/888kJ; Protein 10.3g; Carbohydrate 26.3g, of which sugars 2.3g; Fat 7.8g, of which saturates 2.7g; Cholesterol 81mg; Calcium 23mg; Fibre 1.6g; Sodium 552mg.

1 Preheat the oven to 200°C/400°F/Gas 6. Wrap the grated potatoes in a piece of muslin (cheesecloth) and squeeze out as much liquid as possible. Discard the liquid. Put the potatoes into a bowl and stir in the beaten eggs, potato flour and baking powder.

2 Cook the cubed bacon in a heavy pan over a medium-high heat, stirring constantly, for 3–4 minutes. Add the shallots and cook for a further 3 minutes. Season.

3 Tip the cooked bacon and shallots into the bowl with the grated potatoes and add the ground caraway seeds and fresh dill. Mix well to combine, then adjust the seasoning.

4 Spoon the potato mixture into an ovenproof dish and bake for 35–45 minutes until piping hot throughout.

5 To make the crispy onion rings, heat the oil in a pan. Put the onion rings in a plastic bag or a bowl with a lid and add the flour. Seal the bag or bowl and shake to dust the rings. Drop them into the hot oil to cook, in batches, until golden and crispy. Lift out using a slotted spoon and drain. Serve the bake topped with the onion rings.

Chopped lean bacon braised with leeks makes a superb tasty filling for this satisfying pie. Here the pie is topped off with puff pastry, although shortcrust pastry would be just as good. Serve it with freshly cooked seasonal vegetables.

LEEK, BACON AND EGG PIE

1 Preheat the oven to 200°C/400°F/Gas 6. Put the oil and bacon in a pan and cook for 5 minutes, stirring occasionally, until the bacon is cooked.

2 Add the leeks to the bacon. Stir, cover and cook over medium heat for 5 minutes until slightly softened, stirring once or twice.

3 Stir in the flour and nutmeg. Remove from the heat and gradually stir in the milk. Return the pan to the heat and cook, stirring, until the sauce thickens and boils. Season lightly with salt and pepper.

4 Tip the mixture into a shallow ovenproof pie dish, measuring about 25cm/10in in diameter. Using the back of a spoon, make 4 wells in the sauce and break an egg into each one.

5 Brush the edges of the dish with milk. Lay the pastry over the dish. Trim off the excess pastry and use it to make the trimmings. Brush the backs with milk and stick them on the top of the pie.

6 Brush the pastry with milk and make a small central slit to allow steam to escape. Put into the oven and cook for about 40 minutes until the pastry is puffed up and golden brown, and the eggs have set.

Serves 4-6

15ml/1 tbsp olive oil
200g/7oz slices rindless lean back bacon, cut into thin strips
250g/9oz/2 cups leeks, thinly sliced
40g/1½oz/⅓ cup plain (all-purpose) flour
1.5ml/¼ tsp freshly grated nutmeg
425ml/15fl oz/scant 2 cups milk, plus extra for brushing
4 eggs
350g/12oz ready-rolled puff pastry
salt and ground black pepper.

Energy 202kcal/842kJ; Protein 13.4g; Carbohydrate 9.7g, of which sugars 4.4g; Fat 12.5g, of which saturates 4.2g; Cholesterol 149mg; Calcium 125mg; Fibre 1.1g; Sodium 592mg

This classic combination of potatoes, onions, apples and bacon is packed inside a pastry crust and would have been typical of the thrifty and filling food that was fed to farm workers at the end of a long hard day in the fields.

BACON, POTATO AND APPLE PIE

Serves 4–5

75g/3oz plain (all-purpose) flour
75g/3oz plain wholemeal (whole-
    wheat) flour
pinch of salt
40g/1½oz/3 tbsp lard, diced
40g/1½oz/3 tbsp butter, diced
15ml/1 tbsp oil
225g/8oz lean bacon, cut into small
    strips
2 medium onions, thinly sliced
450g/1lb potatoes, thinly sliced
10ml/2 tsp sugar
2 medium cooking apples
4 fresh sage leaves, finely chopped
salt and ground black pepper
300ml/10fl oz/1¼ cups vegetable
    stock or medium dry (hard) cider
beaten egg or milk, to glaze

1 Sift the two flours and salt into a bowl and rub in the lard and butter until the mixture resembles fine crumbs. Mix in enough cold water to bind the mixture, gathering it into a ball of dough. Chill for 30 minutes.

2 Preheat the oven to 180°C/350°F/Gas 4. Heat the oil in a large non-stick pan and cook the bacon until crisp. Transfer to a large mixing bowl.

3 Add the onions, potatoes and sugar to the hot pan and brown until beginning to soften. Add to the bowl.

4 Peel, core and slice the apples and add to the bowl. Stir in the sage, season with salt and pepper and mix well. Tip the mixture into a 1.5litre/2½ pint/6¼ cup pie dish, level the surface and pour the stock or cider over.

5 Roll out the pastry on a lightly floured surface to a shape large enough to cover the dish. Brush the edges of the dish with milk or beaten egg. Lay the pastry lid over the top, trim the edges and make a slit in the centre. Brush the lid with beaten egg or milk.

6 Put into the hot oven and cook for about 1 hour, until the crust is golden brown and the filling is cooked through.

Energy 436kcal/1824kJ; Protein 12.7g;
Carbohydrate 42.7g, of which sugars 8.2g; Fat
25g, of which saturates 10.7g; Cholesterol 48mg;
Calcium 43mg; Fibre 4g; Sodium 754mg

SIDE DISHES AND BAKES

The scattering of just a little chopped fried bacon can lift vegetables to another level. As well as traditional combinations such as Brussels sprouts or broad beans with bacon, there are ideas here for other unexpected pairings that work like a dream – the bitterness of chicory is softened with crispy sweet-smoky bacon pieces; honeyed sweet potatoes are counterbalanced by matchsticks of salty rasher. And as a special postscript, the ultimate sweet-salt snacks are tucked in for a final irresistible treat!

Crisp smoked bacon blends splendidly with the distinctive flavour and creamy texture of broad beans in this tasty side dish.

Serves 4

30ml/2 tbsp olive oil

1 small onion, finely chopped

1 garlic clove, finely chopped

50g/2oz rindless smoked streaky (fatty) bacon, roughly chopped

225g/8oz broad (fava) beans, thawed if frozen

5ml/1 tsp paprika

15ml/1 tbsp sweet sherry

salt and ground black pepper

Energy 139kcal/577kJ; Protein 6.8g;
Carbohydrate 8.2g, of which sugars 1.6g; Fat 9g,
of which saturates 1.9g; Cholesterol 8mg;
Calcium 38mg; Fibre 3.9g; Sodium 163mg.

BROAD BEANS WITH BACON

1 Heat the olive oil in a large frying pan or sauté pan. Add the chopped onion, garlic and bacon and fry over a high heat for about 5 minutes, stirring frequently, until the onion is softened and the bacon browned.

2 Add the beans and paprika to the pan and stir-fry for 1 minute. Add the sherry, lower the heat, cover and cook for 5–10 minutes until the beans are tender. Season with salt and pepper to taste and serve hot or warm.

A lovely mixture of textures, the bacon adds a spark to humble Brussels sprouts. Stir-frying delivers a sweet flavour and crunchy bite.

STIR-FRIED BRUSSELS SPROUTS WITH BACON

Serves 4

450g/1lb Brussels sprouts, trimmed
   and washed
30ml/2 tbsp sunflower oil
2 slices streaky (fatty) bacon, finely
   chopped
10ml/2 tsp caraway seeds, lightly
   crushed
salt and ground black pepper

Energy 130Kcal/542kJ; Protein 7g; Carbohydrate 5g, of which sugars 3g; Fat 10g, of which saturates 2g; Cholesterol 9mg; Calcium 40mg; Fibre 4.6g; Sodium 300mg.

1 Using a sharp knife, cut the Brussels sprouts into fine shreds and set aside. Heat the oil in a wok or large frying pan and add the bacon. Cook for 1–2 minutes, or until the bacon is beginning to turn golden.

2 Add the shredded sprouts to the wok or pan and stir-fry for 1–2 minutes, or until lightly cooked.

3 Season the sprouts with salt and ground black pepper to taste and stir in the caraway seeds. Cook for a further 30 seconds, then serve immediately.

Bacon is the perfect complement to the distinctive flavour of chicory. This is a good side dish with roast meat or game or hearty casseroles.

ROASTED CHICORY AND BACON

Serves 4

3 large heads of chicory, about
  675g/1½ lb
pinch of sugar, optional
6 slices rindless smoked streaky
  (fatty) bacon, roughly chopped
3 garlic cloves, finely chopped
150ml/5fl oz/⅔ cup vegetable stock
1 bay leaf
ground black pepper

1 Quarter the chicory lengthways. If it is slightly old and tough, blanch it in boiling, lightly salted water with a pinch or two of sugar for 2 minutes to remove any bitterness, then drain well – this won't be necessary if the chicory is young and tender.

2 Heat a large non-stick frying pan and cook the bacon pieces over a medium-high heat for 3–4 minutes or until they begin to brown. Add the garlic and cook briefly, then transfer on to a plate with a slotted spoon, leaving the fat and juices behind in the pan.

3 Add the chicory to the pan and cook for 3–4 minutes or until it starts to caramelize, stirring frequently. Pour over the stock, add the bay leaf and then return the bacon and garlic to the pan.

4 When the stock starts to bubble, lower the heat and cover the pan with a lid. Simmer for 5 minutes, remove the lid and cook for 7–8 minutes, or until the chicory is tender and most of the stock has evaporated.

5 Remove the bay leaf, then taste and season with pepper (you won't need salt, as the bacon will add enough). Serve hot with a helping of boiled potatoes.

Variation

Just before serving, you can flavour the chicory, if you like, with a sprinkling of fennel seeds or chopped fresh herbs such as chives or dill.

Energy 117kcal/484kJ; Protein 6.8g;
Carbohydrate 6.8g, of which sugars 1.4g; Fat
8.5g, of which saturates 2.9g; Cholesterol 20mg;
Calcium 40mg; Fibre 2g; Sodium 396mg.

Bacon adds colour and extra taste to this side that is especially good with a roast meat or braised fish dish. It is a truly great flavour combination.

BRAISED CELERY AND BACON

Serves 4

40g/1½oz/3 tbsp butter
2 slices (back) bacon, chopped
1 small onion, finely chopped
1 carrot, finely chopped
1 celery head, cut into short lengths
175ml/6fl oz/¾ cup chicken or
   vegetable stock
1 bay leaf
1 parsley sprig
salt and ground black pepper

Energy 256kcal/1070kJ; Protein 8.3g;
Carbohydrate 26g, of which sugars 7.6g; Fat
13.9g, of which saturates 6.6g; Cholesterol 30mg;
Calcium 59mg; Fibre 7g; Sodium 364mg

1 Melt the butter in a large heavy pan, then cook the bacon, onion and carrot until beginning to colour.

2 Add the celery and cook over a medium heat for 2–3 minutes. Stir in the stock, bay leaf, parsley and seasoning and bring to the boil.

3 Cover and simmer gently for about 25 minutes, until the celery is tender and the liquid reduced to a few tablespoonfuls. Serve hot.

The earthy flavour of Jerusalem artichokes is excellent with shallots and smoked bacon or pancetta. This is lovely with chicken, pork or roast cod or monkfish.

JERUSALEM ARTICHOKES WITH GARLIC, SHALLOTS AND BACON

Serves 4

50g/2oz/¼ cup butter
115g/4oz smoked streaky (fatty) bacon or pancetta, chopped
800g/1¾lb Jerusalem artichokes, peeled
8–12 garlic cloves, peeled
115g/4oz shallots, chopped
75ml/5 tbsp water
30ml/2 tbsp olive oil
25g/1oz/½ cup fresh white breadcrumbs
30–45ml/2–3 tbsp chopped fresh parsley
salt and ground black pepper

1 Melt half the butter in a heavy-based frying pan and cook the chopped bacon or pancetta until brown and beginning to crisp. Remove half the cooked meat from the pan and set aside.

2 Add the artichokes, garlic and shallots, and cook, stirring frequently, until the artichokes and garlic begin to brown slightly. Season to taste and stir in the water. Cover and cook for 8–10 minutes, shaking the pan occasionally.

3 Uncover the pan, increase the heat and cook for 5–6 minutes, until all the moisture has evaporated and the artichokes are tender.

4 In another frying pan, melt the remaining butter in the olive oil. Add the breadcrumbs and fry over a moderate heat, stirring, until crisp and golden. Stir in the chopped parsley and the reserved cooked bacon or pancetta.

5 Combine the artichokes with the breadcrumb mixture, mixing well. Adjust the seasoning, if necessary, then turn into a warmed serving dish. Serve immediately.

Energy 341kcal/1481kJ; Protein 10g; Carbohydrate 28g, of which sugars 5g; Fat 23g, of which saturates 9g; Cholesterol 45mg; Calcium 79mg; Fibre 1g; Sodium 511mg.

In the original Welsh dish, potatoes, onions and slices of bacon would have been layered in the cooking pot with water and then cooked over an open fire. Here, a flameproof casserole is put on the hob to brown the chopped bacon and soften the vegetables before stock is added and the casserole is then put in the oven.

OVEN-COOKED POTATOES WITH BACON

1 Preheat the oven to 190°C/375°F/Gas 5. Heat the oil and butter in a wide flameproof casserole, add the bacon and cook over medium heat, stirring occasionally, until the bacon is just beginning to brown at its edges.

2 The next stage is to add the thinly sliced onions to the bacon in the casserole. Cook for 5–10 minutes, stirring occasionally, until the onions have slightly softened and turned a rich golden brown.

3 Add the potatoes and stir well. Pour in the stock and level the surface, pushing the potatoes and onions into the liquid. Season with black pepper.

4 Bring to the boil, cover and put into the hot oven. Cook for 30–40 minutes or until the vegetables are soft.

5 Remove the cover. Raise the oven temperature to 220°C/425°F/Gas 7 and cook for a further 15–20 minutes, until the top is crisp and golden brown. Garnish with some chopped parsley.

Variation Try adding a little chopped fresh sage, shredded wild garlic or leeks, or some grated mature cheese in step 4.

Serves 4

15ml/1 tbsp oil
25g/1oz/2 tbsp butter
8 thick slices rindless bacon, chopped
2 onions, thinly sliced
1kg/2¼lb potatoes, thinly sliced
600ml/20fl oz/2½ cups chicken or vegetable stock (or a mixture)
ground black pepper
fresh parsley, chopped, to garnish

Energy 385kcal/1615kJ; Protein 14.8g; Carbohydrate 48.2g, of which sugars 8.9g; Fat 16.1g, of which saturates 7.1g; Cholesterol 43mg; Calcium 44mg; Fibre 3.9g; Sodium 935mg

Smoky bacon is the perfect addition to these melt-in-the-mouth sugar-topped potatoes. They make an impressive alternative to roast potatoes, as an accompaniment to roast duck or chicken.

GLAZED SWEET POTATOES WITH BACON

Serves 4–6

45ml/3 tbsp butter, plus extra for
　greasing
900g/2lb sweet potatoes
115g/4oz/½ cup soft light brown
　sugar
30ml/2 tbsp lemon juice
4 slices smoked lean bacon, cut
　into matchsticks
large handful fresh flat leaf parsley
salt and ground black pepper

1 Preheat the oven to 190°C/375°F/Gas 5 and lightly butter a shallow ovenproof dish. Cut each unpeeled sweet potato crosswise into 3 and cook in boiling water, covered, for about 25 minutes until just tender.

2 Drain and leave to cool. When cool enough to handle, peel and slice thickly. Arrange in a single layer, overlapping the slices, in the prepared dish.

3 Sprinkle over the sugar and lemon juice and dot with the butter.

4 Top with the bacon and season well. Bake uncovered for 35–40 minutes, basting once or twice.

5 The potatoes are ready once they are tender, test them with a knife to make sure. Remove from the oven once they are cooked.

6 Preheat the grill (broiler) to a high heat. Sprinkle the potatoes with parsley. Place the pan under the grill for 2–3 minutes until the potatoes are browned and the bacon is crispy. Serve hot.

Energy 387kcal/1627kJ; Protein 7.2g;
Carbohydrate 49.5g, of which sugars 26.1g; Fat
19.3g, of which saturates 9.8g; Cholesterol 50mg;
Calcium 49mg; Fibre 3.6g; Sodium 562mg.

Crisp bacon and tasty bacon fat makes this salad, a Belgian speciality, extra satisfying. It makes a fabulous light lunch as well as a pleasing side dish.

POTATO, BEAN AND BACON SALAD

Serves 4

600g/1lb 6oz potatoes, scrubbed
  but not peeled
500g/1¼lb/3½–4 cups fine green
  beans, trimmed
15ml/1 tbsp vegetable oil
150g/5oz smoked bacon, finely
  chopped
1 small onion, finely chopped
90ml/6 tbsp red wine vinegar
salt and ground black pepper
15ml/1 tbsp chopped fresh parsley,
  to garnish

Energy 246kcal/1029kJ; Protein 11.3g;
Carbohydrate 29.3g, of which sugars 5.7g; Fat
10.1g, of which saturates 2.9g; Cholesterol 20mg;
Calcium 60mg; Fibre 4.5g; Sodium 595mg.

1 Boil the potatoes in lightly salted water for 15–20 minutes. Drain them, allow to cool slightly and cut into slices.

2 Meanwhile, cook the beans in a separate pan of lightly salted water for 5 minutes. Drain, rinse with cold water, then pat dry with kitchen paper. Put the beans in a salad bowl and cover with foil to keep warm.

3 Heat the oil in a frying pan and fry the bacon until crisp. Remove the bacon with a slotted spoon and scatter it over the beans. Cover again.

4 Return the frying pan to the heat. When the bacon fat is hot, add the onion and fry for 8–10 minutes until golden brown. Tip the contents of the pan over the beans and bacon, then add the potatoes. Mix gently.

5 Pour the wine vinegar into the frying pan. Boil for 2 minutes, stirring constantly to incorporate any bits of bacon or onion that have stuck to the base. Pour the mixture over the salad. Season and toss to coat. Sprinkle with chopped parsley and serve immediately, while still warm.

Bacon, especially if smoked, makes all the difference to the flavour of the cabbage, turning it into a delicious vegetable accompaniment to serve with a roast meal.

CABBAGE AND BACON SALAD

Serves 4

30ml/2 tbsp oil
1 onion, finely chopped
115g/4oz smoked bacon, chopped
500g/1¼lb cabbage (red, white
  or savoy)
salt and ground black pepper

Energy 151kcal/623kJ; Protein 6.7g;
Carbohydrate 7.4g, of which sugars 7g; Fat 10.5g,
of which saturates 2.6g; Cholesterol 15mg;
Calcium 67mg; Fibre 2.8g; Sodium 452mg.

1 Heat the oil in a large pan over a medium heat, add the chopped onion and bacon and cook for about 7 minutes, stirring occasionally.

2 Remove any tough outer leaves and wash the cabbages. Shred them quite finely, discarding the core. Add the cabbage to the pan and season. Stir for a few minutes until the cabbage begins to lose volume.

3 Continue to cook the cabbage, stirring frequently, for 8–10 minutes until it is tender but still crisp. (If you prefer softer cabbage, then cover the pan for part of the cooking time.) Serve immediately.

Variations
• This dish is equally delicious if you use spring greens (collards) instead of cabbage. You could also use curly kale.
• To make a more substantial dish to serve for lunch, add more bacon, some chopped mushrooms and skinned, seeded and chopped tomatoes.

This rustic quinoa loaf, studded with cooked bacon, is lovely when fresh from the oven. Serve sliced and buttered to accompany soup, or salad.

CHEESE, ONION AND BACON BREAD

Serves 8

225g/8oz/2 cups strong white bread flour
175g/6oz/1½ cups strong wholemeal (whole-wheat) bread flour
300g/12oz/2 cups cooked pearl quinoa
10ml/2 tsp easy blend (rapid-rise) yeast
7.5ml/1½ tsp salt
60ml/4 tbsp sugar
300ml/10fl oz/1¼ cups lukewarm water
15ml/1 tbsp vegetable oil
1 small onion, finely diced
4 slices streaky (fatty) bacon
50g/2oz/½ cup mature (sharp) Cheddar cheese, grated
milk, to glaze

Energy 314kcal/1325kJ; Protein 12g; Carbohydrate 51g, of which sugars 10g; Fat 8g, of which saturates 3g; Cholesterol 14mg; Calcium 103mg; Fibre 3g; Sodium 585mg.

1 Sift the flours into a large bowl, add the cooked quinoa, yeast, salt and sugar and stir to mix. Make a well in the centre and gradually mix in enough lukewarm water to form a soft dough.

2 Knead for 6–8 minutes, on a floured board, by holding the dough with one hand and stretching it with the palm of the other hand. Turn the dough and repeat this action, to stretch the dough and activate the yeast.

3 Cover the bowl with a damp cloth and leave in a warm place for 1–1½ hours, until nearly doubled in size.

4 Meanwhile, in a frying pan, heat the oil and add the onion, frying for 4–5 minutes until soft but translucent.

5 Add 2 of the bacon slices to the pan and fry for a further 3–4 minutes, until brown and crispy. Snip the cooked bacon slices into small pieces with some kitchen scissors. Set aside.

6 When the dough has risen, knock back (punch down) and knead for a further few minutes by hand, or with an electric dough hook. Add the bacon, onion and three-quarters of the grated cheese, and fold in and knead just enough to incorporate.

7 Heat the oven to 200°C/400°F/Gas 6. Oil a 450g/1lb loaf tin (pan), or a large baking sheet if you don't have a tin. Shape the dough to neatly fill the tin, or shape into a bloomer shape if using a baking sheet. Leave to prove for another 20–30 minutes in a warm place.

8 Brush the top of the loaf with milk and bake for 15 minutes. Briefly remove from the oven and sprinkle with the remaining cheese and 2 bacon rashers. Bake for a further 15–20 minutes, until the loaf is risen and golden, then remove it from the tin. It should sound hollow on the base when tapped. Return it to the oven for a further few minutes if required.

9 Transfer the loaf to a wire rack and leave to cool.

Adding sugar to bacon may seem decadent, but the combination of salty and sweet is a match made in heaven. Try these on your friends: they will be delighted.

CANDIED BACON

Serves 6

175g/6 oz brown sugar
5ml/1 tsp cinnamon
2.5ml/½ tsp cayenne pepper
12 slices unsmoked streaky bacon

Energy 224kcal/936kJ; Protein 8g; Carbohydrate 24g, of which sugars 12g; Fat 12, of which saturates 4g; Cholesterol 33mg; Calcium 23mg; Fibre g; Sodium 637mg.

1 Preheat the oven to 190°C/375°F/Gas 5. Mix together the dry ingredients and place in a shallow bowl. Line a rimmed baking sheet with parchment paper or foil and place a wire rack on top.

2 Coat both sides of the bacon in the mixture and bake carefully for about 10 minutes, making sure the sugar doesn't burn. Turn the bacon over and bake again for a further 5 minutes.

3 Serve immediately or cool and keep in an airtight container to sprinkle on salads, add to soups, or mix into cupcakes and breakfast muffins.

Popular all over America, bacon dipped in chocolate is the ultimate sweet and savoury snack. A sprinkling of chopped nuts adds extra texture.

CHOCOLATE-COVERED BACON

Serves 4

8 thick slices unsmoked streaky (fatty) bacon
450g/1 lb good quality milk or dark (semisweet) chocolate
chopped nuts, for sprinkling

Energy 742kcal/3104kJ; Protein 18g; Carbohydrate 71g, of which sugars 70g; Fat 45g, of which saturates 24g; Cholesterol 52mg; Calcium 42mg; Fibre 0g; Sodium 847mg.

1 Grill (broil) the bacon until it is crispy. Drain the fat, let the bacon cool then pat both sides with kitchen paper to remove any lingering fat.

2 Melt the chocolate in a double boiler, or in a heatproof bowl set over simmering water. Holding a strip of bacon at the top, carefully dip most of it into the melted chocolate.

3 Lay the chocolate-dipped bacon on a tray covered with baking parchment. Sprinkle the chopped nuts on top. Repeat until the bacon is used up. Refrigerate the tray to set the chocolate.

INDEX

First published in 2014 by Lorenz Books
an imprint of Anness Publishing Limited
108 Great Russell Street, London WC1B 3NA
www.annesspublishing.com
www.lorenzbooks.com; info@anness.com

© 2014 Anness Publishing Limited

If you like the images in this book and would like to investigate using them for publishing, promotions or advertising, please visit our website www.practicalpictures.com for more information

A CIP catalogue record for this book is available from The British Library

Publisher Joanna Lorenz
Editorial Director Helen Sudell
Designer Nigel Partridge
Introduction written by Carol Wilson

Recipes contributed by: Pepita Aris, Catherine Atkinson, Alex Barker, Ghillie Basan, Georgina Campbell, Maxine Clark, Penny Doyle, Matthew Drennan, Brian Glover, Carole Handslip, Valentina Harris, Christine Ingram, Silvena Johen Lauta, Mowie Kay, Lucy Knox, Janet Laurence, Sally Mansfield, Ewa Michalik, Janny de Moor, Anna Mosesson, Carol Pastor, Anne Sheasby, Mirko Trenkner, Linda Tubby, Suzanne Vandyck, Jenny White, Biddy White Lennon, Carol Wilson, Jeni Wright, Annette Yates

Printed and bound in China

COOK'S NOTES

- Bracketed terms are intended for American readers.
- For all recipes, quantities are given in both metric and imperial measures and, where appropriate, in standard cups and spoons. Follow one set of measures, but not a mixture, because they are not interchangeable.
- Standard spoon and cup measures are level. 1 tsp = 5ml, 1 tbsp = 15ml, 1 cup = 250ml/8fl oz.
- Australian standard tablespoons are 20ml. Australian readers should use 3 tsp in place of 1 tbsp for measuring small quantities.
- American pints are 16fl oz/2 cups. American readers should use 20fl oz/2.5 cups in place of 1 pint when measuring liquids.
- Electric oven temperatures in this book are for conventional ovens. When using a fan oven, the temperature will probably need to be reduced by about 10–20°C/20–40°F. Since ovens vary, you should check with your manufacturer's instruction book for guidance.
- The nutritional analysis given for each recipe is calculated per portion (i.e. serving or item), unless otherwise stated. If the recipe gives a range, such as Serves 4–6, then the nutritional analysis will be for the smaller portion size, i.e. 6 servings. The analysis does not include optional ingredients, such as salt added to taste.
- Medium (US large) eggs are used unless otherwise stated.

PUBLISHER'S NOTE